D1718654

In the BELLY of the DRAGON

A Zen monk's commentary on
the *Shinjinmei* by Master Sosan (d. 606)

Volume One

Rei Ryu Philippe Coupey

translated from the French
and edited by
Elaine Konopka

with a preface by
Richard Collins

American Zen Association
New Orleans
www.nozt.org

2005

Taisen Deshimaru

Rei Ryu Philippe Coupey

I dedicate this book to my master, the sitting dragon.

I wish to thank Robert Livingston
and his editor Richard Collins for making this book available
to the American public;
and my disciple, Elaine Konopka, for her invaluable work
and support.
Let thanks also go to my disciple Jean-Pierre Romain.

Contents

Cover photo: interior of a mokugyo (percussion instrument in the shape of a dragon-fish, used to accompany chanting in Zen ceremonies) © emk 2004 www.zen-road.org. Typesetting and layout: Plamen Arnaudov

Preface

From the moment we pick up any English version of the *Shinjinmei* of Sosan (Seng Ts'an, d. 606), we are already tangled in the nets of translation. Neither of the two favored translations of the title, "Faith in Mind" or "Trust in Mind," is adequate; each has its strengths, each its weaknesses; and even both together do not do the trick. First there is the problem of the Chinese conflation of Mind and Heart (*hsin*). But let's assume that the Western estrangement of the two halves of this "not-two" spiritual organ, its decay or falling away into specialized parts, can be overcome in a leap of the poetic imagination à la William Blake, so that feeling and thinking are one, automatic, natural, spontaneous. There remain in the title the separate connotations of Faith versus Trust. To choose "Trust" over "Faith" is a bow to the secular mind of America ("In God We Trust" is on the money: God as reliable business partner or benevolent banker). "Faith," though, labors under an unavoidable load of piety, a suggestion of theism (faith with an object, anathema in Zen practice). So neither term satisfies. Yet combining the two into a title something like "Faith/Trust in Heart/Mind" would be just a barbaric coupling and multiplication of dualities; like the gender-avoiding pronoun creations "he/she" or "s/he," such slashing recreates and reifies more of the very duality it attempts to overcome.

How, then, do we solve this Faith/Trust dichotomy? If we grasp the poem, we should not *solve* this dichotomy, nor *resolve* it, but *dissolve* it. For as soon as we begin to sort out the semantic subtleties, we are entangled—in cultural assumptions, political constructions, religious implications, linguistic contortions, logical reductions. The entire thrust of the *Shinjinmei* is to go beyond these structures of dualistic thinking so that there be no petty squabble between Trust and Faith, just as in Zen practice there be no bickering between Heart and Mind.

Such dualities are resolved only experientially—in zazen.

A similar argument can be made when we begin to look at the origin of the text of the *Shinjinmei*, asking, as we should of all such texts, about its attribution and its authenticity. These are interesting textual questions and should be explored by religious and literary scholars (for the complexity and background of these issues, see Mu Soeng, *Trust in Mind: The Rebellion of Chinese Zen*. Boston: Wisdom, 2004). But Taezen Maezumi made an excellent point, entirely in the spirit of the *Shinjinmei* itself, when he dissolved these textual questions with the fact of its favorable reception—and citation—over the centuries: "The masters' frequent references to the poem have authenticated it as a genuine expression of the spirit of Zen" (quoted in Dennis Genpo Merzel, *The Eye Never Sleeps: Striking to the Heart of Zen*. Boston: Shambhala, 1991, xvii).

The true test of a Zen text, it seems, is not its origin or authenticity but its serviceability. It helps if the style is succinct and suggestive, the better to be passed down orally, like koans, but it must in the end go beyond the beautiful, the entertaining, the instructive; it must above all be useful in the everyday practice of Zen training. Whoever actually wrote the *Shinjinmei*—and there is some question whether it is from the brush of Sosan—this relatively brief poem set the standard for all Zen texts to come in terms of the sheer ordinary usefulness of its pronouncements.

Each strophe restates the first in a bravura performance of 73 permutations. It doesn't matter: any part of an authentic Zen text will, in the manner of DNA, identify the whole. Lift a speck of dust and you lift the world. Grasp the first bodhisattva vow—*shujo muhen seigen do*: "*However innumerable sentient beings, I vow to save them all*"—and you grasp them all. Grasp the opening strophe—"Entering the Way is not difficult, / But you must not love, or hate, or choose, or reject"—and you grasp the essence of the *Shinjinmei*. The net that entangles also lifts us up.

What, then, is the test of a text like Philippe Coupey's *In the Belly of the Dragon*, a comparatively voluble commentary by a contemporary Zen monk on the most ancient Zen text? By its nature, a commentary will be less succinct and more expansive, more explanatory, and perhaps more serviceable by showing its relevance for today. Coupey shows the *Shinjinmei*'s relevance again and again, as he emphasizes the principle of "not-two." In an interview published in *ZenBulletin*, Coupey explained the relevance of the poem this way:

> I, for example, cannot call myself a detached man. Maybe Sensei [Deshimaru] took this position, or maybe Sosan would have taken it. But who are we kidding? Of course I'm attached: I fall in love, I have money problems, I'm always running for something—a train, a plane . . . . I'm always in the tumult of daily life. And I think that's a good thing: from there, true, deep and authentic satori can appear. Because we're not protected. We're in the wind, like a tree on the edge of a cliff that could fall at any moment. We always have this impression that we're going to go completely crazy because of the life around us, the attachments . . . the suffering . . . . And if we can find satori in such a situation, for me it's a very strong satori.

To find satori in the tumult of daily life is one of the hallmarks of the Deshimaru lineage, which avoids many of the monastic constraints of Zen practice and encourages lay practice in the dojo next door. For Coupey, this accessibility is also the essence of the *Shinjinmei*:

> The strength of this poem, its direct quality, is particularly well suited to practice in the Deshimaru lineage. In other practices—and even in other Zen schools, including Soto Zen—there is a lot of talk about progress and degrees. We hear this all the time—but not in the teaching of Kodo Sawaki and Taisen Deshimaru. Our practice is to achieve satori here and now. (Strophe 4)

When asked in the *ZenBulletin* interview "Who is in the belly of the dragon?" Coupey answered: "WE are! The person reading the book is in the dragon's belly." Some people will mistakenly call the book by the title that inspired it, "In the Belly of the Beast," by Jack Henry Abbott. But in the East the Dragon is, traditionally, the vigorous cosmic energy that comes from deep within. So the Dragon of the title is both inside and outside—inner power (*joriki*) and outer power (*tariki*)—because, again, these are *funi* ("not-two").

Newcomers to the New Orleans Zen Temple are often surprised to find that we are not teetotalers or vegetarians. They bring their preconceptions about Buddhism, their misconceptions about Zen. If life's complexities sometimes appear to be simplified by Zen, it is not by exclusion or reduction. Zen, says Coupey, uses everything: words, shouts, meat, alcohol, slaps, everything. Do not choose, do not reject, do not discriminate. Do not cling to your veggies, your smokes, your meat, your ideas, your words, your non-words.

This message has come down to us in ten thousand ways, yet it is still misunderstood. How many koans restate the same idea? In the Soto tradition, koans are used on an ad hoc basis, without having coalesced into a curriculum; koans are, we might say, the literary heritage of Soto Zen, its lore. Many Soto dojos use lectures (*teisho*) as their primary mode of teaching; the edited and reworked lectures of Shunryu Suzuki in *Zen Mind, Beginner's Mind* are a famous example. Instead of koans or teisho, the Deshimaru lineage uses kusen as the primary way of verbally transmitting the teachings. More or less spontaneous oral teachings during zazen, kusen are, we might say, this lineage's calligraphy, written on the air, sometimes recorded, sometimes transcribed, but originally and naturally composed in the medium of breath.

How then should one read the transcription of an oral record like *In the Belly of the Dragon*? It is helpful to know that these kusen were delivered over a period of some eight years, during many sittings, at many sesshin, to many different students, in many different dojos in France and Germany. The book should probably be read—as it was "composed"—not at a single sitting but over time, in fragments to be digested piecemeal and not as the snake swallows its prey, whole.

Also, these chapters should be considered "talks" rather than writings, to be "received" rather than read, to be "absorbed" rather than thought about. To hear kusen while sitting in zazen is very different than hearing a lecture or reading a book. During zazen one's concentration is focused not on the words or voice of the speaker of the kusen, but on the kusen's subject, which is ultimately always zazen itself. In the case of these kusen, the subject of the focus of zazen is identical to the subject of the *Shinjinmei*; the subject is not the *Shinjinmei* itself, which is only the finger pointing at the moon. To hear kusen during zazen is, in this sense, nothing more than an encouragement to focus on concentration itself: it is, perhaps, a little like hearing a lecture on your experience of the Grand Canyon while you are actually *in* the Grand Canyon, rather than hearing a lecture delivered before or after on the rim. Zazen itself shows us all we need to know about zazen, but we can always use the assistance of a geologist who can identify the ancient strata of the canyon wall we're gazing at, or a park ranger who can tell us a good story or two about the early explorers of that old, natural abyss.

Kusen are the calligraphy of the Deshimaru lineage. Kusen are not sermons; they do not offer discourses of spiritual use to the listener. It would be more accurate to compare kusen to *zuihitsu*, the indigenous Japanese literary form that plays on a theme by "following the brush." But the *zuihitsu*, for example, of the fourteenth-century monk Kenko in his *Essays in Idleness* are just that, "essays." Kusen are not essays, not "attempts" like Montaigne's or "meditations" like Loyola's. Kusen are spontaneous oral teachings that illuminate the dojo, like an ember of kodo (incense) drawn on the semi-darkness. They can take the form of exhortation as a single word ("Concentrate!") or a phrase ("Head presses the sky!"); or they can become a poetic essay as deep and firmly structured as the posture of zazen itself.

Reading Rei Ryu Philippe Coupey's commentary, I am, oddly, reminded of the apparently very different kusen of my own master, Robert Livingston Roshi, Coupey's brother monk for many years in Paris under their master Taisen Deshimaru. Yet their kusen styles could not be more different. Robert Livingston's kusen have been increasingly pared down to the bare bones of the teaching, the essential, the germ of the practice, so that his approach is very direct and less verbal, almost anti-intellectual in the American vein. Philippe Coupey's approach, on the other hand, is voluble and literary in the French tradition, allusive, full of explanations and asides, allusions, theories, quotes and anecdotes. I am reminded of Ihab Hassan's book *The Literature of Silence*, which contrasts the volubility of Henry Miller with the reticence of Samuel Beckett, two postmodern voices with the same effect, a tendency toward getting at the truth of what is offered in the ambiguity of silence, which is another Way of talking about the Way that cannot be talked about. Whereas Miller sets out to exhaust language, Beckett pares it down to ellipsis and mime. The kusen voices of Philippe Coupey and Robert Livingston, too, are strong, distinct, yet essentially the same, and contained in the chant of the Dragon himself, for if we listen carefully, in each case, it is the voice of Master Deshimaru coming through.

Richard Collins
New Orleans Zen Temple
December 2004

Shinjinmei
Verses on Faith in Mind
by Master Sosan

1
Entering the Way is not difficult,
But you must not love, or hate, or choose, or reject.

2
If you feel neither love nor hate,
Your understanding of the Way will be clear and penetrating.

3
If a distinction as minute as a particle is created in the mind,
An infinite distance immediately separates sky and earth.

4
If you achieve satori here and now,
The idea of right and wrong will no longer enter your mind.

5
The struggle between right and wrong in our conscience
Leads to a sick mind.

6
If you cannot penetrate the source of things,
Your mind will exhaust itself in vain.

7
The Way is round, at peace and perfect, wide as the vast cosmos,
Without the slightest notion of rest or rupture.

8
In truth, because we want to seize or reject,
We are not free.

9
Do not run after *shiki*
And do not dwell on *ku.*

10
If your mind remains tranquil,
It vanishes like a dream.

11
If you stop all movement, your mind becomes tranquil,
And afterwards, this tranquility will provoke movement again.

12
If you dwell on extremes,
How can you understand One?

13
If you do not concentrate on the original,
The merits of both extremes will be lost.

14
If you accept only one existence, you will fall into that single existence.
If you become attached to *ku*, you will turn yourself against it.

15
Even if your words are correct, even if your thoughts are exact,
It is not in accordance with the truth.

16
Abandoning language and thought
Will lead you beyond all places.

17
If you return to the original root, you touch the essence.
If you follow enlightenment, you lose the original source.

18
If you are enlightened in all directions, even for an instant,
It is superior to ordinary *ku*.

19
Change in ordinary *ku*
Requires the birth of illusions.

20
Do not seek the truth;
Simply be free from prejudice.

21
Do not dwell on opposites.
Do not seek out dualism.

22
If you still have the slightest notion of right or wrong,
Your mind will sink into confusion.

23
Two depends on One;
But do not be attached, even to One.

24
If no mind appears,
Phenomena will be free from error.

25
No error, no Dharma;
No Dharma, no mind.

26
Following the object, the subject vanishes;
Following the subject, the object collapses.

27
The object can be fulfilled as a true object through its dependence
    on the subject.
The subject can be fulfilled as a true subject through its dependence
    on the object.

28
If you wish to understand subject and object,
In the end you must realize that both are *ku*.

29
A *ku* identical to both
Includes all phenomena.

30
Make no distinction between subtle and gross.
There are no sides to take.

31
The substance of the great Way is generous.
It is neither hard nor easy.

32
People with narrow minds will sink into doubt.
The faster they want to go, the slower they will be.

33
If you adhere to a petty mind, losing all measure,
You will veer onto an erroneous path.

34
If you express it freely, you are natural.
In your body, there is no place to go and stay.

35
If you trust nature,
You can be in harmony with the Way.

36
Sanran opposes the truth;
Kontin escapes from it.

37
The mind that escapes from the truth is troubled.
So what is the point of being partial?

38
If you wish to go by the sole and supreme vehicle,
You must not hate the six impurities.

39
If you do not hate the six impurities,
You can attain true buddhahood.

40
The sage is inactive;
The fool loves and attaches himself.

41
There is no differentiation in the Dharma;
But the fool attaches himself.

42
Using mind with mind:
Great confusion, or harmony?

43
In the state of doubt, *sanran* and *kontin* arise.
In the state of satori, love and hate do not exist.

44
You want to think too much
About the two aspects of all elements.

45
Your life is like a dream, a ghost, a flower of emptiness.
Why should you suffer to grasp this illusion?

46
Gain, loss, true, false:
Please, abandon them.

47
If the eye never sleeps,
All your dreams will vanish.

48
If the mind makes no discriminations,
All beings in the cosmos become one.

49
If your body profoundly realizes One,
You can instantly cut all relationships.

50
If you consider all existences with equanimity,
You will return to your original nature.

51
Once you examine this,
You cannot compare it to anything.

52
If you stop movement, there is no more movement.
If you set stillness in motion, there is no more stillness.

53
Since two is impossible,
One is as well.

54
Finally, in the end,
There is neither rule nor regulation.

55
If mind coincides with mind,
The seeds and traces of actions vanish.

56
Since the fox's doubt does not exist,
Passions completely disappear, and suddenly true faith appears.

57
All elements being impermanent,
They leave no trace in the memory.

58
Illuminating your inner self with the light of emptiness
Does not require the power of the mind.

59
As far as *hishiryo* is concerned,
It is very difficult to consider.

60
In the cosmic world of reality as it is,
There is neither ego-entity nor differences.

61
If you want to realize One,
It is only possible in Not-Two.

62
In Not-Two,
All things are alike, beyond contradictions.

63
Sages and all of humanity
Go towards the teaching of the original source.

64
The original source being beyond time and space,
One instant becomes ten thousand years.

65
Neither existence nor non-existence,
Everywhere before your eyes.

66
The minimum is identical to the maximum;
The borders between places must be erased.

67
The largest is identical to the smallest;
Boundaries are invisible.

68
Existence is non-existence.
Non-existence is existence.

69
If this is not so,
You must not protect it.

70
One is all things,
All things are One.

71
If this is so,
Why is it necessary to think about the not-finished?

72
Faith in mind is Not-Two.
Not-Two is faith in mind.

73
Finally, the path of language will be cut off,
And past, present and future will not be limited.

1

Entering the Way is not difficult,
But you must not love, or hate, or choose, or reject.

If you want to know what Zen teaches, there it is, summarized in two lines. In the first line, Sosan is referring to Buddhahood, our Buddha-nature; in the second, he explains what makes us able to see it—or not. Buddha-nature is the nature we all have, even before birth, even after death. Buddha-mind. The mind of rocks. The mind of the Way.

Following the great Way is not at all difficult: trees grow in it, fish swim in it. We all follow it—even when we make mistakes. The Way is right in front of our eyes, right under our noses and under our zafus. And this has not changed since ancient times, since Bodhidharma, since Buddha, since before Buddha.

"From ancient times down to today," writes Master Jiun, himself an ancient, "the great Way has not changed. It is." Then he adds, "The head on top, the legs below to either side." It's a little like when Master Dogen returned from China and was asked, "What have you discovered about Buddhism?" He replied simply, "Eyes horizontal, nose vertical."

This is not difficult at all. But understanding and practicing it is not so easy. *Entering the Way is not difficult.* Sure. But we could also say, "Entering the Way is not easy."

Trees follow the Way; rivers, rocks, birds and fish follow it. For them, it's not hard. But for human beings, it's not always easy, because of "small mind," the mind of selection and choice. With your personal mind, your personal consciousness, your preferences, your desire to stay in bed when everybody's getting up, you can become complicated. You're looking for love, you want to be spoiled: "I like the zazen posture, but not the ceremonies, or *samu*—why should I do *samu*? I want to relax."

There are people who have been practicing for twenty years with this attitude. They're wasting their time. They'd be better off going bowling. Other people see the dojo for the first time, get into zazen posture, hear the bell, and their lives are changed forever. But for people who don't even know that the Way exists, it's very difficult. Very difficult also for those who know that the Way exists but have no idea of how to go about it. So they turn towards Tibetan Buddhism, Hinduism, the Church, Zen, Sufism, macrobiotics, New Age practices. There are many roads you can follow, but going from one to another makes the practice of the Way very difficult.

❧

But you must not love, or hate, or choose, or reject.

The second line explains what blocks us on the path, what hinders us. It means don't select, don't take this and reject that, don't love this and detest that. That's the essence of this strophe: no egotistical love or egotistical hate; no blind love or blind hate.

Love is very quickly transformed into its opposite. People kill each other every day because of love which has turned into hate. There's also admiring love: you love someone but don't dare approach him; you think he's out of your reach. Society functions a lot along these lines—with celebrities, for example. The same goes for love based on understanding: "I understand, therefore I love." "I understand the benefits of zazen, so I practice it." All of this is relative love, just one side.

In mondos, there are always questions concerning love. But which love are we talking about? It's rarely the love that transcends the you/me duality, the love that Master Deshimaru called compassion. We could also call it wisdom. It's the love beyond man and woman, beyond human and buddha.

You shouldn't confuse the two: small love and cosmic love; narrow love, based on you and me, and love that does not rely on you or me—a love that can blossom even within the couple. This love or compassion takes place when there is no difference between man and woman, before the thought "he's a man, she's a woman" appears. Before any thought. Before small mind arises.

But that's not what Master Sosan is talking about in the first strophe of the *Shinjinmei*; he's talking about small, everyday love: love for my girlfriend, for my wife, for myself; love based on attachment to the six senses—sight, smell, hearing, touch, taste and consciousness. That love is not at all necessary; it makes life complicated. It can even make you crazy. We've all experienced it, and if not, we dream of encountering it. Of course, you can still live in a couple, beyond egoism. *You must not love* doesn't mean don't love; it means study the right way to love. Ask yourself, "How should I be with someone? How should I love?"

No choice or rejection means not choosing with your personal consciousness, and also not choosing your thoughts. We're always busy picking and choosing. Even in classical meditation, we choose our thoughts—we choose to meditate on good thoughts rather than bad ones. Before I encountered zazen, I practiced a little Hindu meditation; we meditated on the beauty of the sunset, or on universal love. This has nothing to do with Zen practice. During zazen, we don't pick our thoughts; we don't assign them a value; we don't say, "This thought is better than that one." Whether we're thinking about sex or Buddha, it's the same thing: they're thoughts, *bonnos*, illusions.

In everyday life—at work, for example—you obviously have to choose your thoughts. But this happens automatically. If you're cooking in the kitchen, you're not making scientific calculations, and vice versa. In daily life, people follow the Way unconsciously, even if they don't know about zazen. Otherwise, life becomes very difficult, and you find yourself endlessly confronted with choices: "Should I go to sesshin or not?" "Should I stay or should I leave?" Practiced this way, the Way becomes difficult.

On the other hand, as Sosan writes, if you don't fall into this dilemma of choosing and rejecting, the Way is not difficult. When you do a sesshin, you follow the sesshin without thinking too much. You get up with everybody else, you do zazen, you eat *genmai*. That's following the Way.

Master Sosan is saying that practicing the Way is not difficult if you are *mushotoku*—not trying to get anything. Of course, in the beginning, it's normal to want to obtain something. You come

21

to the dojo for years, you go to sesshin, you set aside time and money for the practice, you put aside your personal affairs, you put aside your family, your wife and children are waiting for you at home. And why? To get nothing? It may seem absurd. So inevitably you want to get something in exchange, or at least come home glowing. But even that doesn't always work. Sometimes you want to show you're serene and wise. You come home after three days of zazen . . . and right away there's a fight!

As a practitioner, it's hard to see if you're progressing. Often, you might even have the impression that you're regressing. When you're on top of the wave, you see the horizon; you feel like you're advancing. But later, when you find yourself in the crook of the wave, you can't see anything and you think you're regressing: all you can see is the wave. It's a matter of perspective—the view from above, the view from below.

If you practice for ten or twenty years, you have some perspective on those ten or twenty years and you see a progression. If your ego is making the choices, you see only the superficial side: you earned money, now you have the car and the house, you're better off than you were before. But if it's not your ego making the choices, you see something else. That's why the master's reply to the disciple is often, "No, there is no progress." The master is talking to the person's ego.

It's obvious that something changes in our lives thanks to an authentic practice. But it's impossible to grab hold of this fact, to focus on it, to say, "That's it!"

Practicing with a goal is like trying to catch a feather with an electric fan. Wanting to get something—wisdom, or satori, for example—is making a separation between *samsara* (a life of transmigration) and nirvana (satori). And in the beginning, it's true, you think there's a difference between the ordinary person and Buddha, between *bonnos* and satori. Everybody thinks that way. But these are ideas that block our perception and understanding. Because satori lies beyond the choices of the conscious mind. In the final analysis, choosing and rejecting are only ideas, distinctions that you make. And in the end, it is this life of selection that is difficult: being obliged to choose, always feeling that you have to choose.

But if you practice Zen—zazen—then the Way is not difficult. Zazen is the perfect illustration of not-difficult, of not choosing. For example, try understanding zazen through books. You have to start by choosing the books. And this booklearning very quickly becomes complicated and hard, whereas the study of Buddhism and Zen through zazen is very simple. When zazen becomes simple, you stop comparing yourself with other people, or even with yourself, to see whether or not you're making any progress. Life inside the dojo, and also daily life outside of it, becomes simple, and you easily manage to harmonize with all things. You're no longer bowled over by your emotions, by love, hate, choice or rejection.

Finally, this Way, this splendid and wonderful Way, is perhaps neither easy nor hard, neither internal nor external. Don't empty out your head; don't fill it up, either. Don't create an inside; don't create an outside.

Nose vertical, eyes horizontal: this is the practice of the Way.

If you feel neither love nor hate,
Your understanding of the Way will be clear and penetrating.

The second strophe of the Shinjinmei is a confirmation of the first: if you do what is said in the first strophe—in other words, not choosing, not always putting your preferences first—then your understanding of the Way will be clear and penetrating.

The Chinese kanji (ideogram) for "clear and penetrating" is the image of daylight when it enters a cave. A literal translation gives us the following:

Do not have either good or bad thoughts.
You will have spontaneous understanding, clear as the light
which enters a cave.

Here is my own version:

If you feel neither love nor hate,
The understanding of the Way will blind you with its obviousness.

Obvious, like the moon reflected by the water.

But the image of the cave has more nuance than this. There is a metaphorical sense: nothing provokes the light that enters a cave. It's the same for understanding and the mind. Master Deshimaru said, "'Cave' also means entering the cave or entering the mountain, in other words, becoming the mountain." He translated the second line more literally: "Your understanding of the Way will be as clear as daylight entering a cave."

৽

Neither love nor hate. "Love" in the sense of chasing after; "hate" in the sense of running away from.

Many people do not understand *Neither love nor hate*. When Master Deshimaru came to Europe, this teaching raised a lot of questions. People found Zen quite severe, and not very compassionate. Master Deshimaru did not realize the extent to which we Westerners cared about our loves—girlfriends, boyfriends, friends, etc. He didn't understand that love is an everpresent criterion for us. In this respect, it's a good thing that some masters today are Westerners: they're in a position to respond to this type of question.

We shouldn't retreat into ourselves, into our personal loves, our personal hates. This only creates subjective complications. The self should be empty of its own self. Yet some people do just the opposite. They're so caught up in their own world that even zazen practice can't get them out. Masters often deal with people who are imprisoned by endless personal problems. It's because they're always going from thought to thought, and have been doing so for a long time.

Neither love nor hate means freeing yourself from stupid attachments. If you're attached, you're not free, and your mind loses its purity. You notice this all the time, especially if you practice zazen.

So don't run away. Don't look for anything. Don't be attached. Not being attached certainly seems difficult, but it means: be free, available, everywhere. That way, you can be attached to everything freely—to human beings, birds, insects—without complicating your life.

For me, this means, "no attachments," or rather, "don't be handcuffed by attachments." One master said, "You must be detached, always detached, and even more detached." In other words, detach yourself from the sense organs. Don't be attached to what you see or hear. You must feel and understand with your body, not just with your eyes and your head. Don't be taken in by the senses, don't be attracted to beauty, don't be repulsed by ugliness.

If you look at an object or a person and feel attachment or love at that moment, then you fall into the devil's snare. In Zen teaching, it is always said that we should not let ourselves be abused by the demons of sight, smell, touch, etc., and that we should not become prisoners of sex, food or the environment. Don't be attached to lovely metaphysical Buddhist sayings, either. Don't be attached to words: "The master said it, so that's how it is." To avoid this, things are often phrased negatively in Buddhism, so that you don't fall into the word trap. You must not run after the masters' words, or follow them to the letter, but follow what the masters followed instead. They're two very different things.

It's like the image of the monk Hotei pointing to the moon with his finger. You shouldn't look at the finger (the word), but at the moon. This may seem obvious, but it's not.

There was once a hermit named Senrin. One day, a friend came to visit him and slept in his hut. The next day, Senrin wanted to give him a gift. He took a block of stone and transformed it into pure gold. Naturally, the friend in question was very impressed. A block of gold! But he quickly grimaced. So Senrin figured maybe he wanted a second one. He pointed his finger at another rock, which immediately changed into gold. But the friend was not any happier.

"I give you two blocks of gold and you're still not happy. What do you want?" asked Senrin.

"I want your finger!" screamed the friend.

☙

Love, in the sense of attachment and dependence, distances us from the Way. Love is very beautiful, love for your wife, for your husband. But it makes life complicated.

The love that Sosan is talking about is personal, subjective love, which shuts you up in yourself and creates major complications. It's not about compassion, but something exclusive that is just for you. You mustn't be too attached to this love, nor to the happiness or unhappiness it brings—because happiness always goes hand-in-hand with its opposite. Some people are attached to happiness, others to unhappiness. It's a reflection of the ignorance which afflicts all of us to some degree.

I think we can love without falling into the attachment trap. But to do this, we must understand what attachment is. This understanding is essential. Attachment is thinking that the object of your attachment—a woman or a man, for example— is a real object with substantial existence. This is an illusion: we are continuously changing. We are not what we were yesterday, nor what we will be tomorrow. Everything is transient. We are change itself. But because of attachment, we grab hold and we can't let go anymore, we can't forget. We're always thinking, "She's not the same person anymore. She doesn't respect me the way she used to." Well of course—she's not the same person anymore! Neither are you! Neither am I! We change all the time. So what do we attach ourselves to in the end? To the past. That's the problem.

Yet it is possible to love without being blindly attached. You have to be careful not to get caught up in yourself, with your personal feelings, always subjective. No one is above this, and it's an occasion to look at yourself: "She loves me—she loves *me*—but who am I?"

❧

When you receive the ordination, you don't reject your family; you cut your attachment to them and go towards something higher. This doesn't mean that you refuse the love of your wife or husband or children. It's the exclusivity that you're cutting: "I want to protect my wife and children. But that one over there isn't my child, so I'm not interested, he can do what he wants. I only have one child, not ten thousand." But that's exactly the point: why not have ten thousand?

It's a classic error to think that your children belong to you. Your children have come from the sky, from heaven, for a moment. Your house and furniture too. Every thing and every human being has a life of its own. Nobody belongs to anybody. Everything, absolutely everything, is a gift. Everything is received from the sky and returns to the sky. And everything that comes to you comes only for a moment

Even the painting an artist creates, or the book she writes, no longer belongs to her once the work is finished. She may have the copyright, but the work is no longer hers. Anyone who creates has the almost physical feeling that they're not doing the creating: they are simply a channel through which creative energy passes. But for this energy to circulate freely, you must not have personal ideas—no love, or hate, or preference—because they only block the way. With this mind, you can paint or write masterpieces, because it is no longer the small self that is producing.

Everything has its own life: the person you love, the child that supposedly belongs to you, the painting, the book, the objects. It is important to understand this profoundly. And if you can understand it in your bones, in your *hara*, then you can live in peace and have compassion for everything: other people, animals, objects, and even the air you breathe.

⚬❈⚬

In the end, Neither love nor hate brings us to *funi*, not-two. Neither this nor that means not-two. But not-two is not beyond the interdependence of things. Sosan is talking about the love and hate that go together.

In 676, Master Eno left his retreat with fishermen in southern China and went to Canton, where he walked by the temple of the Nirvana School, which is not very different from Zen. A few monks were talking about a flag waving above their heads. One said, "The flag is moving." Another, "No, the wind is moving." And Eno said, "Mind is moving." The monks were very impressed.

That's the classic version of the flag story, the one found in Paul Reps' book[1] and other collections of Zen stories. But according to Master Deshimaru's version, the first monk said, "The flag is moving," the second monk said, "No, it's the wind," and the third monk, Eno, replied, "No, it's consciousness that's moving." At that moment a nun who was

---

[1] Paul Reps and Nyogen Senzaki, ed., *Zen Flesh, Zen Bones: A Collection of Zen and Pre-Zen Writings* (Boston: Tuttle, 1989).

passing by overheard the discussion and said to the other three, "No. You are all mistaken. Everything is moving: flag, wind and mind."

Neither love nor hate. That means, don't fall into contradictions and duality. (Is it the flag or is it the wind? Unless it's the mind?) It's another way of saying that we have to stop discriminating between good and evil. Not-good-or-evil. No need to choose, no need to reject. Not-good-or-evil and immediately the Way appears before you.

"When you think of neither good nor evil," said Eno to Domyo, "what is your true face, your true self?" Eno's question has become a famous koan.

Eno worked in the kitchen of Konin's temple, in charge of the mortar used to crush the rice. He practiced zazen on the *gaitan*, since he was forbidden to enter the dojo on the grounds that he was uneducated and could neither read nor write. Eno received the transmission from Master Konin, even though everyone thought it would go to Jinshu, the most cerebral, best educated and most scholarly of all the disciples. The other monks were furious, especially General Domyo, who set out in pursuit of Eno. Following the advice of Konin, who feared the other monks' jealousy, Eno had fled in the night, as soon as he had received the transmission. Domyo, who was traveling on horseback, caught up with Eno in two days. Eno placed the bowl and the kesa—the emblems of the transmission—on a rock and hid behind a bush. He thought the general would content himself with these objects and give up the idea of killing him. But when Domyo went to take the bowl and the kesa, he couldn't lift them, because they had suddenly become very heavy. The general was furious. Eno came out from behind his bush and asked, "Why have you come? For the Dharma, or for the bowl and the kesa?" "For the Dharma, of course," replied Domyo. "I have come for the Way! Please, transmit it to me." And it was then that Eno pronounced the words: "Think of neither good nor evil. At this moment, what is your true face?"

There are other interpretations of this question; for example, "Without thinking about what is true or false, seek your face before the birth of your parents." One version by Master Deshimaru says, "You, Joza! Without thinking of good or evil: who are you?"

All the masters have expressed themselves on this matter. Ikkyu, a fifteenth-century Japanese monk, wrote this poem:

My old self, which never originally existed,
Has nowhere to go after death, absolutely nowhere.

Not-good-or-evil. Be beyond. This practice is the Way.

3

If a distinction as minute as a particle is created in the mind,
An infinite distance immediately separates sky and earth.

All Zen masters have studied the *Shinjinmei*, and their disciples have too. Since Sosan composed it, many other masters through the centuries have referred to the strophes of this poem in their own writing: Sekito in the *Sandokai*, Yoka Daishi in the *Shodoka* and Tozan in the *Hokyozanmai*, as well as other Soto masters such as Fuyodokai, Wanshi, Dogen, Keizan, Daichi, Menzan, Kodo Sawaki and Taisen Deshimaru; and in the Rinzai School, Mumon Ekai in the *Mumonkan* and Engo Kokugon in the *Hekiganroku*.

For example, here is what we find in the second paragraph of Master Dogen's *Fukanzazengi*: "If the slightest gap exists, the Way remains as distant as the sky from the earth."

Master Deshimaru's comments on this strophe come down to this: "If a gap of a hairsbreadth is created in our minds, the Self no longer coincides with the ego, nor the mountain with the mountain." Even though Master Deshimaru talked a lot about the ego, he never said that we should get rid of it. He was even known to criticize religions that tried to crush the ego, to always make it smaller: "My ego's smaller than yours!" Master Deshimaru said, "My ego is bigger. I have a super ego—it is as vast as the cosmos."

❧

Don't make distinctions. That's what the first three strophes of the *Shinjinmei* are talking about. By separating the sky and the earth, we create a division in our own minds. So don't have any seeds inside you. Let nothing grow! Neither for nor against. As soon as you show the slightest preference or the slightest antipathy, your mind is divided and lost in confusion.

One day Master Maezumi asked his disciple Genpo, "Are you a vegetarian?"

Genpo replied, "I never eat meat."

"Do not be attached to any philosophy or any thought," said Maezumi.

The same question was asked of Master Dainin Katagiri.

"Are you a vegetarian?"

"A tiny little bit," he replied.

No separation, no distinction. But this doesn't mean that we raze the mountains and fill up the valleys. It is simply about mind, big mind, and how this mind quickly becomes very small. Running after the *shiho* (Dharma transmission), running away from the *shiho*—that's small mind, the mind that makes distinctions.

Master Deshimaru said that we shouldn't try to attain anything. I suppose he meant that the result isn't important. It's not like a contest, where the arrow has to hit the middle of the target. The arrow is shot exactly, and that's all that matters.

The practice is what's important, exact practice. It is said that we must cultivate the Way. I don't like the term "cultivate"; I prefer "take care of." In order for a tree to grow, it has to be able to drink through its roots, so water must be able to penetrate the ground. That's why you loosen the soil around a tree. That's taking care of it. And it's identical to the attention you give to the practice of the Way. You go to the dojo, you go to sesshin, you study.

You must always take care. Because today, you make a small distinction; tomorrow, that distinction will take on larger proportions. A particle in the mind, a speck of dust, an atom . . . and the error becomes infinite.

One night I was sailing my father's boat, which was going to Corsica. I was navigating by compass. In the morning, we found ourselves in Baléares, hundreds of miles off course. A mistake is a mistake; there's no "almost." A drop of ink in a glass and the water isn't clear anymore. Just one particle and the sky and earth are separated. Missing the target by an inch is the same as missing it by a mile. Anyway, there is no target.

What's important is climbing the mountain, not the view from the peak. Sometimes people climb to the top of a mountain, and once they're up there they can't see anything because of the clouds. Then they think they've missed something.

Wanting to get something is entering into the dualistic world. But that world exists, and sometimes it's necessary to want to obtain. So, how do you know when you should and when you shouldn't?

Wisdom, which is not separate from compassion, can show us what is or is not necessary to do. Not ordinary wisdom, but *maka hannya* (*maka*, "great"; *hannya*, "wisdom"). A wisdom that is neither particularly human nor particularly inhuman, but which comes from *ku*, which comes, quite simply, from nothing.

❧

In this strophe, Sosan talks about *a distinction as minute as a particle*. This concerns the thinker, the person who discriminates. Just a tiny notion of right or wrong, and you become confused, or, as Sosan puts it, you "separate sky and earth." The sky and the earth cannot be separated; one cannot exist without the other. Sosan is saying that thinking complicates everything. "This lovely flower is blooming for me. This fly is annoying me." Separation.

Don't create the particle that will put an infinite distance between the sky and the earth; don't wind up in hell. Hell is not a place: it's a state of mind. Making distinctions means creating hell and heaven, because separation creates heaven just as surely as it creates hell. As soon as you start making choices, you're adopting the perspective of the ordinary person, who thinks there's an awakened human being on one side and an ignoramus on the other.

Some religions don't seem at all bothered by this separation. On the contrary, they like it. It has the advantage of simplifying things: if you're good, you go to heaven; if you're bad, you go straight to hell. But according to Buddhist teaching, heaven, hell, all that is in your head; it's made of thoughts.

Of course, everything also depends on your point of view. If your point of view is high and your perspective wide, then there is no creation of distinctions at all. "The master, the Buddha, speaks to me directly." That's the religious mind *par excellence*, as when Buddha said, "I alone am awakened." Here, no more distinctions, no more separation between sky and earth. From the point of view of an awakened person, everyone is awakened; everyone has Buddha-nature. Originally, fundamentally, everyone is awakened. Our true natures are in perfect harmony with the cosmos. Our true nature is calm and peaceful, and we should all discover what we've always had inside us.

But where does the master place himself when he declares that an awakened person sees everyone as awakened, whereas the non-awakened person makes the distinction between the man of satori and the man of *samsara*? Does the master consider himself awakened or not?

I think the awakened person simply does not see himself in these terms. Words are a form of communication that we should leave behind us like a raft once we have crossed the river.

4

If you achieve satori here and now,
The idea of right and wrong will no longer enter your mind.

We can see every strophe of the *Shinjinmei* as an explanation of what satori is, or what it isn't. Such is the case for the fourth strophe.

This translation is by Master Deshimaru. Another version, by Richard B. Clarke, reads:

> *If you wish to see the truth,*
> *Then hold no opinions for or against anything.*[2]

But "to see the truth" is not as concrete as to *achieve satori here and now.*

We might also say, "If we achieve the Way here and now, everything appears before us and our conscience is pacified."

The strength of this poem, its direct quality, is particularly well suited to practice in the Deshimaru lineage. In other practices—and even in other Zen schools, including Soto Zen—there is a lot of talk about progress and degrees. We hear this all the time—but not in the teaching of Kodo Sawaki and Taisen Deshimaru. Our practice is to achieve satori here and now. Only here and now, and that way, there is no more wrong, no more right in the mind.

According to Sosan, we are not walking on the Way as long as we are driven by judgments such as right or wrong, for or against. Master Deshimaru talked a lot about the suffering which results from these opposites. He often said that if we abandon our ideas of right and wrong, everything appears before us and our conscience is pacified.

So if you want to see the truth, do not take a stand for or against anything. Anyway, "for" becomes "against" and "against"

---

[2] Cited in Dennis Genpo Merzel, *The Eye Never Sleeps: Striking to the Heart of Zen* (Boston: Shambhala, 1991), p. 127.

becomes "for." We've all experienced this: wanting something but being unable to obtain it, we change our attitude, we stop loving, and we start hating.

Of course, sometimes you must take a stand. But you can do it naturally: take a stand without taking a stand. If you put water in a round container, it takes the shape of a round container; if you put water in a square container, it takes the shape of a square container. And yet water is always water. This means, don't force things in one direction or another, this way, that way, to the north, to the south. Do not choose.

❧

One day, Master Tozan asked his monks a question. The shusso thought he was able to reply, but he had to give ninety-six answers before Tozan finally said, "Why didn't you say that sooner?" I don't know if the shusso really gave all ninety-six answers during the same mondo. In any case, he gave ninety-six answers and the ninety-sixth was the right one. He had satori.

Another monk, the tenzo, had heard all the answers except the last. He began to harass the shusso. "What was the ninety-sixth answer?" But the shusso refused to answer him—and he was right to do so, since the answer itself wasn't really what was important. Nevertheless, for three years the tenzo remained obsessed by this affair and he continually asked the shusso to tell him the ninety-sixth answer. But still the shusso refused.

One day, the shusso became ill and was bedridden. The tenzo went into his room and said, "For three years I've been asking you politely to tell me what you said. Now I'll have that answer by other means." He pulled out a knife and said, "Give me the answer or I'll kill you!"

The shusso was very frightened. He was sick in bed, and his hands were under the covers; there wasn't much he could do. So he said, "All right, I'll tell you!" Then he added, "But you know what? Even if I tell you, you still won't have what you're looking for."

Suddenly, the tenzo understood. He put away the knife and did *gassho*. He had satori. He no longer needed the ninety-sixth answer.

If you think the answer is here or there, you will never understand.

❧

Master Deshimaru explained the fourth strophe this way: "If our mind and our conscience are at peace, always tranquil here and now, we can preserve this state of tranquility. Without it, we cannot be happy."

"If our mind is tranquil here and now..." But how does this happen? Through zazen, obviously.

Zazen is finding your original nature, which is completely different for each of us, yet at the same time similar for everyone. This original nature is absolute tranquility. And what is absolute tranquility? I think it is faith, faith with no objective.

Tranquility lies within faith; it is something that slips in and becomes engrained in everything, in all the nooks and crannies of our daily life. Master Deshimaru used to say that if our mind is in a state of true tranquility, neither failure nor misfortune can cause suffering.

Naturally, everyone has moments of tranquility. In fact, everyone struggles in his own way to obtain tranquility. You work hard to be able to go home and finally have some peace. But I'm not talking about that tranquility, which disappears as soon as you find yourself in a difficult situation. I'm talking about the tranquility of the person who is aware of his original nature.

"Unconsciously" is a word that Master Deshimaru used often; but "unconsciously" does not mean unaware. An awakened master is "unconscious" as a tree is unconscious, or a mountain. And he is something more as well. He is awakened. He knows.

Recently I read a passage by Master Wanshi. Wanshi was a great practitioner of zazen, in other words, *hishiryo*-consciousness (*hi*, "beyond"; *shiryo*, "thinking"). In this passage, he says that when there is nothing in our mind, nothing special, we know there is nothing. And if we do not know, it is Zen-disease and not true Zen. Wanshi talks about "transparent mind." It's not correct to say there's nothing there, because transparent mind is there.

When you walk, you know you're walking, even if you're totally concentrated on the walking itself. When you sleep, there are several ways to sleep: there's the person who falls into bed like a sack of potatoes; others fall asleep but somewhere remain awake—not exactly conscious but not unconscious either. They are really asleep, but they also have a mind that stays out of sleep, a light mind, which doesn't fall asleep for or against, and doesn't wake up for or against either.

⁓⁓⁓

So don't think in terms of for or against anymore, right/wrong, good/evil, low/high, sacred/profane. Don't complicate your mind. Don't complicate things. Don't complicate your own life, or other people's lives. Because all of it, in the end, is just ideas, opinions and personal thoughts; and that's what weighs the most, that's our heaviest baggage.

Master Dogen said in the *Shobogenzo* that our possessions, our thoughts and our opinions are not real. They are dependent on karma. So put down your baggage. Be light, don't carry any unnecessary baggage; don't carry any baggage at all. The higher you want to go, the more you have to leave everything behind, and go naked.

Be profoundly tranquil, natural in every situation. Be yourself. And that doesn't mean having a personal point of view. Here and now, simply find your original nature.

Be like the tiger entering the forest, or the dragon penetrating the sea. For the tiger, the forest is home; he is protected there, he cannot be shot at as on the plains. He is no longer hunting; he is entering the forest. It can be the same when you enter your own home and are naturally yourself. And it's the same for the dragon. And the monk getting into the posture is also, at that moment, going home.

5

The struggle between right and wrong in our conscience Leads to a sick mind.

The fifth strophe is fairly simple to understand; it is completely connected to the fourth and responds to it.

Just, unjust: most religions pit one against the other, and "just" becomes "justice," which becomes punishment. But in Buddhism, this duality does not exist. This is why Sosan says *the struggle between right and wrong in our conscience leads to a sick mind.*

Right, wrong, for or against: from this inner struggle between desire and rejection, from this for-or-against which permeates the mind, sickness is born. For example, the person we love doesn't love us—immediately, we start hating them. This is one of the symptoms of a diseased mind, at an advanced stage. We've all experienced it.

Master Deshimaru said, "Do not create differences, do not follow anything, do not fight, do not look for God or Buddha, do not run after the Dharma. All of this causes sickness in the mind. We must cut off all things. We must cut the ten thousand relations, we must not imagine anything, but not destroy anything either. The fruits of feelings of love and attachment are desire and hate." All masters of the transmission speak this way.

Don't create differences between yourself and others, don't make yourself sick by looking at them with a judgmental eye which establishes categories or follows a line of conduct. It's not necessary to analyze, to see if a certain person or thing is good or bad; we're all both good and bad. Sometimes Master Deshimaru criticized his disciples, but it was never a judgment—you can immediately recognize someone who doesn't judge. It was always to awaken our true nature, our original nature, the Buddha-nature we can see if we look at ourselves. And with the practice, we wind up seeing this original nature in others as well. Then we begin to see them differently; there is no more for, against, good or bad ... no more sick mind.

৵

What we suffer from the most is too much thinking. Following a particular behavior or system of thought creates inner conflicts. And this disease, this purely mental suffering, creates neurosis.

Sometimes people who are beginning zazen practice suffer quite a bit physically. In zazen, the muscles (which are in fact in their normal state) work in a way which is different from how they work in ordinary life. They hurt due to lack of practice. And the best cure for the physical pain of zazen is obviously to practice more zazen. But when you stop hurting physically, sometimes an even greater suffering appears—that of the mind. Your mind hurts, you stagnate in your thoughts, you get sick.

Almost a thousand years ago, Master Fuyodokai said, "Monks should hate the dirty work of the mind, be beyond life and death, stop the activity of the mind and reject all complicated relationships." "Complicated relationships" refers to human relationships, but also to the activities of our conscience.

The problems which existed in Fuyodokai's time were not so different from ours, except that today they're much worse. Why? Because things become more pronounced with time. You shoot at a target placed a yard away, and you miss by an inch. Put the target ten thousand yards away, and you miss by a mile. Today, mental suffering is far greater than physical suffering.

Master Deshimaru, who liked to talk about our civilization, often said that we have become weak, weaker than ever, and that we find ourselves defenseless. In the subway in Paris, the advertising billboards often target people who suffer from stress rather than physical pain—stress which comes from problems within the couple, from daily agitation, from noise, from professional concerns, from the need to earn a living. And this anxiety leads to a sick mind. That's why zazen is so important today.

Zazen is observing your thoughts. But this does not mean observing the chain of thoughts. In fact, when you observe thoughts, their connection is broken. Observing means observing the birth and death of a thought, and in so doing, freeing yourself from it. You observe a thought; it dies and leaves room for another thought, which is transformed into non-thought as it dies in its turn.

And so zazen is observing life and death. Observing *mujo*, impermanence, change—the very idea of which is often the cause of illness. In Zen, it is said that everything is change, that there is nothing but change; but we could also say that there is no real change, that change is only apparent, that it is limited to form. Someone who is completely detached, who is not driven by his ego, can easily understand this. It's true—what changes, really? The packaging. The essence does not change.

Letting your thoughts pass, without stopping them: that's all you have to do, today and tomorrow, for one year, five years, ten years. Because if you practice observation this way, all inner conflicts, all mental sickness disappear. The mind returns to its normal condition, and your original Buddha-nature appears. Then you achieve the Way in the here and now.

"Do this for ten years," said Master Joshu, "and I promise you, you will find the Way. Otherwise, you can cut off my head and use it as a washbasin."

6

If you cannot penetrate the source of things,
Your mind will exhaust itself in vain.

The fifth strophe explains that if your brain works too hard, it becomes sick. The sixth tells us that if you don't penetrate the depth of things, beyond dualistic categories like good and evil, your mind also becomes sick.

This strophe contains the kanji *gen*, which means "the origin," "the source of things," "the source of existence." This means that if we don't know the deep meaning of things, we are needlessly disturbing our original mind.

Master Deshimaru explains that the original principle, deep nature, is not a product of our six senses—six including consciousness—and that the sixth strophe is talking about a world beyond consciousness. In deep nature, he adds, there is neither dualism nor monism. As Fuyodokai said, not the left head or the right head (dualism), or the head in the middle (monism). Here, Master Deshimaru is talking about the man who is surprised by his shadow (we could also say image). Sometimes people run after their shadow, sometimes they want to escape it. The shadow is only a phenomenon. Yet many people think it is true happiness.

Another translation of Strophe 6, by Master Sheng-yen, says that we should recognize "the mysterious principle."[3] Mysterious because deep nature has nothing to do with our eyes and what we see, with our ears and what we hear, with our mind and what we think. It is, in fact, a world beyond consciousness: the invisible world.

Through the practice of zazen, we become sensitive to the invisible world, we come into contact with it: the half-dead, the half-alive, the *pretas* and *devas*. And we come into contact with the original source: non-desire, or *ku*.

---

[3] Master Sheng-yen, *Faith in Mind: A Guide to Chan Practice* (Elmhurst, NY: Dharma Drum Publications 1987), p. 21.

In China, under the T'ang Dynasty in the 800s, Raisan (nicknamed "the farting master") lived in the plains where he grew sweet potatoes. He was a great Zen master, and famous in his time, even if only one anecdote is known about him. We don't even know if he had any disciples—apparently you don't always need disciples to be a master, even a famous one.

The emperor, who had heard about Raisan, wanted him to come pay a visit, because he wanted to get some information about Zen. So he sent a messenger to Raisan with the mission to bring him back. An entire retinue of noblemen from the palace accompanied him. They arrived at the monk's hut, in the middle of a field, at lunchtime. The messenger knocked on the door, saying "Open up! I am the emperor's envoy! He is waiting for you and my mission is to bring you back to the court."

Raisan was eating a sweet potato. When you eat sweet potatoes, you fart a lot, and so he was doing exactly that. He didn't answer the emperor's messenger. It wasn't the right time. It was lunchtime. The messenger said, "If you do not come, I will take back your head without your body." This did not disturb Raisan in the least.

The messenger finally decided not to bring Raisan's head back to the emperor, but to return to the palace and tell him the story. When he heard it, the emperor, furious, cried, "Bring him here this instant! I want to hear him speak about Zen!"

So the messenger went off again to Raisan's hut. It happened to be lunchtime again. He knocked at the door and shouted, "Open up! This time I will bring back your head if you refuse to come with me!" But Raisan ignored him and continued to eat his sweet potato.

The messenger walked around the outside of the hut and looked through an opening that served as a window. From there he saw Raisan eating a sweet potato. "Open up. The emperor wants to see you right away." No answer. The messenger was dumbfounded. He could have killed Raisan. That was when he noticed that the monk's nose was running. The snot was dripping down his mouth and onto the sweet potato. "Hey, Master, your nose is running," he said.

"So what?" answered Raisan. "I'm eating."

The messenger once again gave up on cutting off his head. Perhaps he had understood something. Anyway he accepted this answer and set off homeward. When he arrived at the palace, he told the emperor how Raisan had not wiped his nose because he was eating. The emperor burst out laughing and said, "All over the world, people think it a great honor to meet me. But not this master."

And so the emperor issued a decree which protected Raisan's sweet-potato fields. He had the neighboring field purchased without the monk's knowledge, so that he could continue to farm his potatoes in utter tranquility for the rest of his days.

This is a true story. It's about non-desire, about *ku*, the great void, the origin of all things.

If you cannot penetrate the source of things,
Your mind will exhaust itself in vain.

If you can understand what is original, *ku*, then complications will cease to arise in your consciousness and in your life. If not, things become complicated in your head. Some people practice for years and become more and more complicated. You ask yourself, "Why is this person, who has practiced for twenty years, even more stupid than before?" You tell yourself, "Maybe it's because he doesn't have deep karmic roots. Maybe he doesn't have faith." But in that case, you should *pretend* to have deep karmic roots, you should *pretend* to have faith—because, in my opinion, you have to start somewhere. You put on a black robe, for example; you do zazen; and then during the ceremony, you concentrate on *gassho* and think about Buddha; during *sampai*, you hit your head hard on the ground. This will surely bring you more wisdom, and more faith as well.

No need to be strong or profound to practice zazen. Maybe we become so. But when the ego's functioning stops, a human being becomes a human being, a tree becomes a tree, a mountain becomes a mountain.

What do you become when you practice zazen? You become normal. You just come back to the normal condition.

7

The Way is round, at peace and perfect, wide as the vast cosmos,
Without the slightest notion of rest or rupture.

The Way is round. Round like the cosmos, round like the universe, round like the earth, round like the moon, round like the sun, round like the eye that sees. Not long or short. Round. In *La Rondeur des jours*[4] (*The Roundness of Days*), Jean Giono writes, "Days do not have a long shape, the shape of things which move towards goals, an arrow, a road, the human race; they have a round shape, like the sun, the world, God."

The Way does not have the shape of things which move towards a goal either, like an arrow shot into the sky, like a road, like the human race.

The Way is round could mean, for example, that it has no beginning or end. It is always said that things begin now and finish later. The day begins... But when did the day begin? At what point in time? And when exactly does it end?

There are many translations of this strophe. They all say, "The Way is perfect." Only Master Deshimaru's says *The Way is round*. Round like Buddha, round like God. Master Deshimaru said, "round like *ku*." Not big or small, but round like a pea, round like the earth.

The Way is round, at peace and perfect, wide as the vast cosmos

The vast cosmos does not mean "nothing," or "emptiness," but rather "everything," which is also *ku*. However, although the vast cosmos includes everything, it is in no way a matter of individual, personal existence. It is not metaphysics, it is not psychology and it has nothing to do with what we like or don't like.

---

4 Jean Giono, *La Rondeur des jours* (Paris: Gallimard, 1970).

Without the slightest notion of rest or rupture.

One day, a young woman told me that she was very troubled because she thought her zazen practice was not exact. But even that's just a lingering thought. Even if you can't breathe well, it's the Way; even if your posture is twisted, it's the Way. We never think or say, "That tree is imperfect," or "That tree is not manifesting its original nature." In a dojo, who is not manifesting his or her original nature?

Without the slightest notion of rest or rupture means that there is nothing missing and nothing extra.

When he received the transmission from Bodhidharma, Eka, the second patriarch, understood that wanting to get something leads nowhere. You get something you absolutely want and you're happy, but not for long; afterwards, you want something else, because in the final analysis you see that you didn't actually get anything the first time.

And when he received the transmission from Eka, Sosan understood that it is futile to reject anything at all. Even if you succeed in rejecting something—a great desire for someone or something, for example—the desire doesn't necessarily disappear from your head.

The practice of the Way is not that of the social world—getting, getting—and it does not consist in rejecting the world, either. We don't even reject our thoughts, not even "bad" ones. We all have thoughts; that's okay, as long as they go away—in other words, as long as we don't try to hold onto them or reject them.

The Zen monk is called *shukke*, "out of the house," one who has left home. But that doesn't mean he falls into a black hole. He will always live somewhere. What has he left, then? He has left the thought of home—no set thoughts, no set home.

This means that every place is your home. No need to live outdoors, in a ditch, in a hole or in a monastery. No need to go to Japan to look for the Way.

The Way is not something outside yourself, something outside your mind.

The Way is round. It is everywhere.

8

In truth, because we want to seize or reject,
We are not free.

Do not run after anything, do not run away from anything. This is a teaching often heard from all the masters and it is also the theme of the first strophes of the *Shinjinmei*. Here again, Master Sosan is talking about dualism, about duality and non-duality. It's a recurring subject which Sosan develops throughout the *Shinjinmei*.

∽❦∾

Because we're always wanting to seize or reject, we don't perceive the true nature of things, so much so that we're not free, and of course we suffer.

In Buddhism, this suffering is expressed by the image of the wheel of life, whose movement hurls people by turns into the six states: *gaki*, the world of insatiable desire; *asura*, the world of violence and aggression; *chikuso*, the animal world; *naraka*, hell; *shomon*, the human world of personal satisfaction; *deva*, the world of the gods.

For example, if you are greedy, you may become obsessed with money, or sex, or power. You can't get enough. You become like a *gaki*, always wanting more, and it's impossible to find peace. From this state of desire and greed, you fall into violence, the world of the *asura*. You're angry with people who have more than you, aggressive with people who come between you and your desires. Then, you become like an animal, *chikuso*; you're suffering so much from your desires that you maybe even kill someone. So you fall into *naraka*, you go to prison. There, you're filled with regret and you promise yourself you'll change. This returns you to *shomon*, the human state. You reflect on your experience. You write a book about it. It's a best-seller. It's picked up by a Hollywood producer and gets made into a movie. You're on top of the world, feeling very satisfied with yourself. You're like a *deva*, everything's great.

But soon desires arise again.

Each state can span a lifetime or a few years. Some people experience all of them in a single day. Whatever the case may be, in general the cycle continues until death.

In most Buddhist texts and schools, what I've just explained is taught in dualistic terms, in terms of the negative-positive opposition associated with the law of causality: "Because I do this, I become that." The action of this law of causality can be observed everywhere; after the cold comes the heat, and, eventually, the cold again. There's no end. It's the same for people: pleasure/pain, love/hate, *mushotoku/shotoku*....

❦

Buddhism, especially Zen, teaches us the importance of the present moment. Here and now, who are you?

This is how we can become free from moment to moment. And this true freedom is *inmo*, "like this." Dogen said, "*Inmo* is body and mind in the eternal present." The body and mind of the eternal present.

This strophe has nothing to do with philosophy, and the comments I am making on it are not at all abstract. It has to do with our lives here and now, our relationship to others—our relationship to our supervisors during *samu* or at our jobs; the relationship between leaders and those who follow them; and finally our relationship to ourselves during zazen.

Sosan's words apply to all of us: we are not free, we are not *inmo*—hence our agitation. Why? Because most of our thoughts are thoughts of desire and selection—"I like, I don't like." Almost everyone functions this way without even realizing it. Always thinking about the past, for example, is not *inmo*. Neither is thinking about the future. And yet we devote a lot of time to this kind of rumination.

A person who is not free functions as if in a sort of dream. When you're sleeping, you don't know you're asleep.

✌

To explain the eighth strophe, Master Deshimaru spoke about *nyorai*, which touches on something we cannot seize or reject. This recalls the first strophe:

Entering the Way is not difficult,
But you must not love, or hate, or choose, or reject.

Through our choices and preferences, we limit our awareness. The small mind wants things for itself; what it doesn't want, it discards. We like pretty flowers, we hate weeds, says Dogen. Sometimes we want to seize, sometimes to reject, and so we are not free. This is no longer connected to the spirit of "suchness"— no more *inmo*, no more "like this."

Do not conclude from this that you mustn't desire anything. The great mind desires what the universe desires. It's a question of "how" rather than "should"—"I shouldn't want to grab onto anything, I shouldn't want power." You should want as the universe wants, you should want as the Way wants. You should want in the right place.

But how do you know what the universe wants?

One day Joshu asked his master Nansen, "What is the Way?"
Nansen answered, "Everyday mind is the Way."
"Should I steer myself towards it or not?"
"If you go towards it, you will distance yourself from it," replied the master.
"But if I do not go towards it, how can I know what the true Way is?" asked the disciple.
"The true Way is beyond knowing or not knowing."

In the end, we must abandon this question of wanting or not wanting, liking or not liking, because, from the point of view of the universe or the Way, there is no separation. We are not separate from each other. What we like and what we dislike are not

50

separate. Nor are pretty flowers and weeds: they're "like this," *inmo.*

Master Dogen explains that *inmo* means grass, trees, tiles, stones, the four elements, the five *skandha*; he says that this is all just mind, a single mind, in other words, true form—*inmo.*

Diversity becomes One. One is diversity. Essence is One, not two. Love is two, compassion is One. And the greatest compassion is to love the weeds too, with no separation.

❧

Master Tokusan is famous for his motto, "Thirty blows if you speak, thirty blows if you're silent." Yet his disciples were often angry with him because they thought he was too gentle and kind.

There was, in his sangha, a real bum, as we say nowadays. Some monks said to Tokusan, "Do you realize that this guy stole money from his father and spent it all on alcohol? He was disinherited by his family and spent a long time in prison."

"Oh yeah?"

And:

"Every chance he gets, he's plotting something, and he steals money behind your back."

In Tokusan's temple, there was a room reserved for sick people. One night, when they were all asleep, the man in question, who had received the monk's ordination, sneaked into the room and stole the sick people's money.

"There, you see, Master? Helping this guy is throwing pearls before swine! He'll eat your pearls and defecate them, and that's all."

Tokusan replied, "He is not a bad man. Sin and sainthood are *ku*. The snake swallows the frog, the toad swallows the worm, the falcon eats the sparrow, the pheasant eats the snake, the cat catches the rat, the big fish devours the little fish and everything is fine. The monk who has offended the precepts does not fall into hell."

9

Do not run after shiki
And do not dwell on ku.

It's a shame that materialistic people aren't spiritual as well. It's a shame that spiritual people aren't materialistic, too.

Do not run after shiki means don't run after phenomena, don't run after conditioned existence, don't be attached. Don't be attached to your thoughts, to your body, to the environment. The country is nice; so is the city.

It's the same for *ku*. Do not dwell on emptiness.

Some Zen practitioners think that everything is an illusion and therefore nothing is important. They practice for years with this perspective and then one fine day they leave. Why do they leave? Because they wind up thinking that even the practice is not important.

On the other hand, other people come to practice to get something: *shiki*, tangible benefits. They immediately get themselves a zafu, a kimono or a kolomo, and get ordained as monks, with a rakusu and kesa. Then they stay another few years. Then they leave. Why? Because in the end, they realize that they haven't gotten anything at all. Sometimes they've actually lost something: their boyfriend, their wife, their job.

These two types are very common and elder disciples see them come and go all the time. In the main reception room at La Gendronnière Temple in France, there's a large photograph which was taken in 1981. One of our favorite pastimes is to look at it and say, "Hey, remember him? Remember her? We never hear from them anymore." At least three-quarters of the people in the photo have completely disappeared. And when you look at a 1973 photo, four-fifths of the people are gone.

What we're practicing here is not a kind of training to attain something. It's not like a university, where you get a diploma and you leave. It's not like some Rinzai practices either, where once you've succeeded in solving a hundred or so koans, the master tells you goodbye. He gives you a certificate and you leave at once, never to return.

Here's a quote from Master Hakuin, a great Rinzai master who died in 1769. In this passage, he uses a somewhat crude vocabulary, but I'm not changing anything; these are his own words:

> The masters of our school have never transmitted the smallest scrap of Dharma to their disciples. Not because the masters were concerned with protecting the Dharma, but because they were concerned with protecting themselves. Today, the disciples who arrive are generally ignorant, stupid and unmotivated. The masters in question instruct these people and treat them with tender care. They might just as well take a heap of cows' heads, line them up, and try to get them to eat. In the end, it's actually a heap of shit that they're stuffing them with, after which they send them back out into the world equipped with duly stamped *shiho* certificates. The difference between them and Isan or Kyogen [two great masters in the Rinzai lineage] is like the difference between mud and clouds.

What we are doing here is an eternal practice. And it's important to stay together, always to practice with other people. Naturally you can change temples or dojos. You can go wherever you want. But wherever you go, don't forget that the practice is for life—for two lives, even. For all lives.

Don't run after *shiki*; don't dwell on phenomena. Don't dwell on *ku* either: emptiness, truth. Don't even have any ideas about *ku*.

Elder disciples are familiar with the story of Gonyo and Joshu. Gonyo was the disciple of Master Joshu, in the ninth century. This story makes him seem like an idiot. Yet he was an authentic disciple. He was very well respected, but he was a little strange. He often walked around with two tigers at his side and a snake wound around his waist.

One day, he went to see Joshu and said to him, "I have come with nothing. What should I do in such a situation?"

Another master, like Obaku or Baso, would have slapped him. But Joshu was very gentle. He told him, "Throw it away."

Gonyo replied, "But I just told you that I've come with nothing. So what do you want me to throw away?"

"Throw it all away."

Don't carry any burdens. Many people who think and say "I have nothing" lead a have-not life. And they carry this have-not with them, even into death.

❧

Most religions seek the truth and want to get rid of illusions. Zen says, neither *ku* nor *shiki*.

Instead, go from *shiki* to *ku*, and from *ku* to *shiki*. Go from thinking to not-thinking and from not-thinking to thinking. This is *hishiryo*-mind.

Shiki sokuze ku. "*Shiki* becomes *ku*." *Ku sokuze shiki.* "*Ku* becomes *shiki*." But phenomena cannot become *ku*, emptiness, vacuity; *ku* cannot become *shiki*, form, phenomena. And yet *shiki* is in itself *ku* and *ku* is *shiki*. It's a koan.

So there's no sense staying on one side or another. Don't fall into the Zen trap. Be flexible. Go with the flow. In the end, abandon even Zen, even Buddhism. As Master Deshimaru always said, we should practice unconsciously, naturally and automatically.

10

If your mind remains tranquil,
It vanishes like a dream.

People who practice zazen experience this.
Here are some other translations of the tenth strophe. First, English scholar R.H. Blyth's version:

If the mind is at peace,
These wrong views disappear by themselves.[5]

The phrase "these wrong views" refers to the preceding strophe, which says:

Do not run after shiki,
Do not dwell on ku.

Translator Richard B. Clarke's version is the best known:

Be serene in the oneness of things,
And such erroneous views will disappear by themselves.[6]

Like Blyth's translation, this means: if you're calm, if instead of running after things you stay in their oneness, if you are simply One, then erroneous viewpoints will disappear.
Master Sheng-yen's version goes in the same direction:

In oneness and equality,
Confusion vanishes of itself.[7]

5 R.H. Blyth, *Zen and Zen Classics*, v. 1 (Tokyo: Hokuseido Press, 1960), p. 63.
6 Merzel, *The Eye Never Sleeps*, p. 28.
7 *Faith in Mind*, p. 26.

If your mind remains tranquil,
It vanishes like a dream.

Tranquil, here, does not mean amorphous, groggy or asleep, but in the normal condition. Master Deshimaru always said "rediscover the normal condition"—in other words, come back to the original state.

It vanishes... "It" means the *bonnos*, the illusions, the problems that we have in our heads. "It" is the mistaken viewpoint, as Sosan says in the ninth strophe, the mind's tendency to run after phenomena or dwell on vacuity (we might even say, "on the truth"). And when the mind functions normally, naturally, automatically and unconsciously, this mistaken viewpoint vanishes like a dream.

This is satori.

Master Keizan said, "The wind dies down, the ocean disappears." Naturally, he's talking about the mind, or about the similarity between reality and the world of appearances. He says that in the mountains, "flower petals fall in silence, everything becomes calm and peaceful." Master Dogen also describes this in a poem: "Thus the wind is calmed, the waves fade." Nothing . . . yet everything.

Satori means losing something, losing the mind that thinks and thinks and thinks. The mind that thinks and thinks is a self-conscious mind. It's like wearing a shoe that's too tight. When your shoe fits, you forget it; you don't walk around saying, "I have a terrific shoe." It's the same with mind.

The same goes for satori: you get it when you don't need it. You get it when you have it.

꿍

Remember the story of Master Tozan's tenzo, who was ready to slit the shusso's throat to get an answer out of him? "Okay, I'll tell you," said the frightened shusso, "but you know, even if I do, you still won't have what you want." The tenzo had satori, put away his knife and bowed.

This is when the mind returns to the normal condition—it disappears. You put away the knife. And there is no mind. *Mushin.*

Everyone's true nature is absolute tranquility. It's *because* of this tranquility, and not in order to obtain it, that we practice zazen. You don't look for fundamental tranquility; you practice it, unconsciously.

Master Dainin Katagiri said that this tranquility is faith. And naturally we can actualize it during zazen—in fact we all do it, more or less. But how can we actualize it, or achieve it, outside of zazen? Simply by always being in the present moment. *Doshu.* And that's exactly where faith is: in the present moment. Faith is the present moment.

We have certainly all experienced this, even before practicing zazen. In fact, maybe that's what brings us to zazen: faith in the universe—faith in ourselves, since we are the universe. But the problem is knowing how not to lose this faith, how not to be affected by doubts and thinking. There are certain methods in which you count breaths, others in which you concentrate on your koan, still others in which you stop your thoughts. It's not like that in the Deshimaru lineage. We don't stop anything at all. We don't begin anything, either. But whatever we do, we do it completely.

Faith is the essential force. With faith, you can understand the *Shinjinmei* and all the other Buddhist writings with no problem. Without faith, they're not so easy to understand.

In Buddhism, faith has nothing to do with what other religions imagine it to be. In most universal religions such as Christianity or Islam, God or Allah becomes the object of faith, an object to which people are very attached. And this way, unity is broken. In Zen, faith has no object. It's not faith in God, or in Buddha, but faith in oneness, beyond God, beyond Buddha. The object of faith and faith itself are not separate. This is non-duality.

It is said in a sutra that faith is "pure awareness." That's what is taught, but whether or not the word "pure" is really understood is another matter. Pure awareness is like *hishiryo*-consciousness.

Pure awareness does not mean suppressing thinking; it's thinking/not-thinking, not-thinking/thinking. It's the normal human condition. It's the "tranquility of mind" that Sosan speaks of.

Perhaps we can establish a similarity between purity and *ku*, emptiness—not the emptiness that contains nothing, but the emptiness from which all things come. People are afraid of emptiness, of *ku*; they're wary of it. That's why Nagarjuna, the great intellectual master of Buddhism (intellectual, but also a zazen practitioner), decided to use the word "purity" instead of *ku*.

Master Ippen of the Shin School goes even further than Zen masters on the subject of faith without object. He says, "Faith is only an action of the mind, and therefore subject to corruption." He practiced faith through total abandon to Buddha Amida. Those who practiced with him abandoned everything and were content to recite the *nembutsu*: "*Namu Amida Butsu, Namu Amida Butsu, Namu Amida Butsu...*" They didn't practice zazen. Ippen taught that one should abandon oneself, not have any mental standpoints, not exert any effort to understand, not try to measure spiritual progress of any kind. For Ippen, religious realization was non-existent. This is not Zen. Nevertheless, it's one way of examining the question of faith using the eyes of faith.

There are several kinds of faith. There's Ippen's faith, which is the most extreme. There's also illusory faith, which we encounter all the time: the irrational devotion of disciples who blindly follow a guru or master. Everything the guru says is true, and if the guru is against something, so are they.

A kind of distantly admiring faith also exists: believing in the teaching, but considering it to be too elevated, inaccessible. Many people experience this kind of feeling about Zen: "Unfortunately, I'm just not ready."

There's also faith based on understanding: understanding with the rational mind. "Buddhist teaching is logical, therefore I believe in it."

And then there's faith received through true knowledge or true experience, the experience of the practice, beyond rationality, beyond all logic. This is the faith Sosan is talking about. Faith is not something we learn from the outside, but something that comes from the inside, from experience.

❧

At any rate, the tenth strophe says that when the mind is at peace, tranquil, in the normal condition, *it vanishes like a dream.* This means being at peace with things just as they are. Unconsciously, automatically and naturally, things are already One.

Does this mean you should just stand there and do nothing? No. You can develop faith in mind, faith in the practice, faith in the fact that we all have Buddha inside us. Faith in yourself is faith in others. To do this, you must first give yourself over to the practice—to continuous practice.

In a dojo, in zazen practice, you sit without moving, you experience the world, you experience yourself, without running after things, without running away from anything, without being influenced by your desires. It's knowing or experiencing the truth of being present now. Sitting in zazen is, in my opinion, the highest experience. Through it, you develop faith in human beings. Whatever you see, you see through faith's eyes. Whatever you hear, you hear with faith's ears.

11

If you stop all movement, your mind becomes tranquil,
And afterwards, this tranquility will provoke movement again.

This means that when you try to stop activity to get passive or calm, that very effort provokes movement. Here again, Sosan is talking about zazen. People set their minds on the tranquility of zazen. The wind dies down, and then what happens? *Bonnos* arise more than ever. At that point, new practitioners often wonder what's going on. Elder practitioners unconsciously understand that illusions come up even more if you try to calm your consciousness. That's one of the differences between beginners and more experienced practitioners of the Way.

In the same way, in the first few years, people try to correct wrong by heading towards right. But later on, they're disappointed and often leave the practice, because this right that they've tried to set up in their lives has turned into wrong.

Master Deshimaru said, "If you want to stop your illusions and attain satori, satori will become an even greater illusion." He also said the following, which I find very profound: "If you start from death and go towards life, that life will be true life. If you want to stop death and you become attached to life, that life will become death."

He also talked about "falling low in order to get back up." Fall in the mud, right to the bottom, and do it with a big exhalation, and that way you can come back up to the surface. He said, "You have to die at least once."

When my co-disciples and I became monks, movement stopped, honors were abandoned . . . but soon, the question of the transmission—the *shiho*—entered our minds, and the tranquility we had known became movement once again. What should we do?

The Way of Zen is both easy and not easy. It's like a tree without roots. Hard for some people to accept. It means always cutting away sentimentality, cutting away ideas of well-being, cutting away the duality with which we are continually confronted in our lives and in the practice.

Master Tozan was walking in the mountains when he came upon an old man doing zazen in a cave.

"Why are you doing zazen this way?" asked Tozan.

The old hermit replied, "There were two cows fighting, two enormous cows, and they were so caught up in their fight that they fell into the sea and were never seen again."

The old man practiced exactly and the two cows disappeared from his consciousness.

This is what having no desire means. Nothing, no mind. *Bonno* and satori are illusion. That's why you must not look for one or the other, but go beyond both of them, beyond movement and tranquility. That's satori, the Middle Way.

12

If you dwell on extremes,
How can you understand One?

Extremes: satori/illusion, good/evil, life/death...

Good/evil. If you want to, you can see evil everywhere. For some people, human beings are bad, hypocritical, egotistical. Other people, on the contrary, see only good—and those people certainly lead a more pleasant life.

Life/death. On one side: our world, the visible, matter. On the other side: the invisible world, the mind. These categories exist only in our thinking.

We only see this or that; we see only one of two extremes. And in so doing, we see only the opposition between things, filtered through our opinions and our viewpoints—because extremes are also a matter of personal choice.

In Buddha's time, there were sixty-two philosophical schools of thought in existence. They were always in conflict, but they didn't clash; they disagreed, but they never resorted to violence. Today, we kill at the drop of a hat. We kill each other because we're black, white or yellow; we kill each other because we're Hindu, Islamist or anti-Islamist.

Why have we become so stupid? I wonder.

❧

So, Sosan tells us, do not dwell on extremes, on concepts, on interpretations.

This may seem obvious, but it's not easy to practice. Not falling into one extreme or the other, not falling into one way of being or the other, not seeing the world through your own concepts—this is what's so hard for ordinary people to do, even those who practice zazen.

Extremes, existence.... Every human being has his or her own personal way of being, but it often becomes erroneous and dogmatic.

During ordinations, the master shouts *"Dai ju fuho sanbo kaifu kyaku gen kai!"* so loudly that his face turns purple. It means, "Do not hold personal, erroneous, dogmatic opinions." It's the tenth *kai*, the last of the monk's ten precepts, all of which come down to us from Buddha's time.

Even though Master Deshimaru regularly reminded us that Buddha and God are not separate, in mondo people often said to him, "My family is Catholic. They don't like the fact that I practice zazen." "This perspective," he would answer, "is one that weakens and shrinks the mind."

There are in fact many Zen stories that perfectly illustrate this "shrunken mind"—for example, the story of Gozu and Master Doshin.

Gozu was thought of as a saint and a wise man, but from a Zen standpoint he wasn't as wise as all that. He lived as a hermit in the mountains. His wisdom was so visible that birds brought him flowers and tigers protected him. Master Doshin, the fourth patriarch, was visiting him. One day, after a mondo they had together, Gozu truly experienced satori. And what happened then? The birds stopped bringing him flowers and the tigers went away.

That's a Soto Zen satori.

In Buddha's time, the sixty-two schools were divided into two branches: *joken*, which asserted that the soul is permanent; and *danken*, which thought that death is the end of all things. These categories or classifications have always existed. *Joken* means "constant, perpetual, eternal"; it's an optimistic position. *Danken*, on the other hand, means that our behavior in the present, whatever it is, has no influence on our future life.

Master Deshimaru talked about *joken* and *danken*. Kodo Sawaki did too. Both of them often repeated that Buddhism had nothing to do with these branches. They said—as did all masters of the transmission and Buddha Shakyamuni himself—that Buddhism is beyond that. Buddha, who studied these two ways of thinking (which Master Deshimaru called "the two prejudices"), stated innumerable times that neither of them was exact or perfect.

But that doesn't mean we should rivet ourselves to a point located halfway between these two extremes. The Middle Way means sometimes going to the right and sometimes going to the left, because the Middle Way includes both.

If we do not dwell on extremes, then we can understand One. The wisdom Sosan is talking about is located in neither one nor the other. We express this wisdom morning and evening in the recitation of the *Hannya Shingyo*. *Maka hannya haramita shingyo* means "Great sutra of the profound, essential, absolute wisdom that goes beyond."

All the masters of the transmission said that the practice of zazen is the best of all paths. This is not an extreme position, but an expression of the master's spiritual certitude. All the great Zen texts teach this non-doubt or non-hesitation. For example: the *Fukanzazengi* ("The Way is fundamentally perfect"), the *Zazenshin* ("Only zazen is realizing, only zazen is doing"), the *Sandokai* ("The smallest doubt causes a separation as great as the distance between the mountain and the river"), the *Hokyozanmai* ("No error, no doubt: such is the Dharma"), the *Hannya Shingyo* ("For the bodhisattva, thanks to this wisdom that goes beyond, there exists neither fear nor doubt").

The man or woman of the Way should go forward without doubt, without hesitation. Then body and mind express the Way. If a master said, "The Way that I practice is okay, but there are others that are better," he would be a very difficult master to follow. He would always be asked which school was the best. "Master, why isn't your school the best? Why is the other better?"

At any rate, being profound in the Way means being profound in every way.

13

If you do not concentrate on the original,
The merits of both extremes will be lost.

The thirteenth strophe, like many other strophes in the *Shinjinmei*, is very difficult to grasp and comment on outside of zazen practice. We can't understand it with discriminating thinking. We can't understand it through language based on concepts, or by reading books, or by listening to lectures—except perhaps during zazen, when the words of the teaching reach our hypothalamus from the master's hypothalamus. But even those who practice may have a very hard time understanding what concentrating on the original means. In fact, because of this, many of Master Deshimaru's disciples left the practice over the years.

Here is how Kennett Roshi, a British Zen master who taught in England and the United States until her death in 1996, translated this strophe:

If you are not conversant with this oneness of mind,
Both your stillness and your activity lose all their merit.[8]

This is an intellectual translation; it implies that if you don't understand the profoundness of the Way, then stillness and activity are both failures.

Now here is an academic translation by Clarke, which is the most widely used version:

Those who do not live in the single Way
Fail in both activity and in passivity, in assertion and denial.[9]

---

[8] Reverend Master Jiyu-Kennett, *The Journal of the Order of Buddhist Contemplatives* (Mt. Shasta, CA: Shasta Abbey Press, 1994), p. 3.
[9] Merzel, *The Eye Never Sleeps*, p. 128.

Master Deshimaru's translation uses *the original* instead of "the single Way." This is an important difference. Sosan is telling us to concentrate on the original, that is, the original mind, the mind from before birth, the mind after the birth of our great-grandchildren. In other words, the eternal present.

When Daibai Hojo was young and practiced with Baso, he was very impressed by a mondo in which he asked Baso, "What is Buddha?"

"*Soku shin soku butsu*—Mind is Buddha," Baso replied.

Hojo had a great satori.

Afterwards, he left Baso and settled on Mount Daibai (which means "big plum"), where he lived as a hermit, almost an ascetic. His only clothing was lotus leaves he had stitched together; his only food, acorns and plums. He practiced alone for thirty years. His only companion was a frog who took to sitting just in front of him when he did zazen. During zazen, Hojo would balance an iron pagoda on his head and had to be careful not to sneeze or cough or fall asleep; otherwise the pagoda would tumble onto his knees, or worse, onto the frog.

One day, Baso asked one of his disciples, "Whatever happened to that nut Hojo?"

The disciple replied, "He's sitting all alone somewhere in the mountains. He's still very impressed by what you told him: '*soku shin soku butsu*—Mind is Buddha.'"

"I don't say that anymore. Now I say '*hi shin hi butsu*—No mind, no Buddha.' Go find Hojo and tell him that."

After searching for a month, the disciple found Hojo on Mount Daibai and announced, "Hey, Hojo! Baso doesn't say '*soku shin soku butsu*' anymore. Now he says '*hi shin hi butsu*.'"

Hojo then replied, "Baso can say what he likes. He can say 'Mind is Buddha,' or 'No mind, no Buddha,' it makes no difference to me. I'm sticking with 'Mind is Buddha.'"

The disciple went back to see Baso and reported this exchange. Baso was very satisfied and said, "Daibai [the big plum] is ripe."

This story shows how Hojo discovered his original face: he understood that he lacked nothing. But of course, this happened after years of practice. If you have not followed in the footsteps of a master, how can you know the traceless path?

෧෫෨

If you do not concentrate on the original,
The merits of both extremes will be lost.

Both extremes is a reference to the eleventh strophe, which talks about stillness and movement, or inactivity and activity. Concentrating on original mind does not consist of concentrating on these two extremes at the same time. It's really about not stagnating in duality; because if you're stagnating in duality, how can you recognize original mind?

At the end of his commentary on the thirteenth strophe, Master Deshimaru says, "If we are not concentrated, at least during zazen, we remain either in movement or at a standstill… Moving and stopping are errors. If we grab on to the two extremes, how can we achieve original mind?"

In other words, activity without tranquility or inactivity without inner activity is erroneous. Zazen is stillness, but it is not stillness within stillness. It is activity within stillness.

For people who have not been practicing for a long time, it's hard to find activity in stillness, and even harder to find stillness in activity. After a sesshin, for example, these people dive right back into activity and their minds go backwards very quickly.

Once I read a newspaper interview with a flamenco dancer. He described flamenco as "alternating hyper-agitation and complete stillness." This is not zazen. During zazen, we are neither in hyper-agitation nor in complete stillness. It's important to be clear on this point. You must not ruminate on your thoughts or imagination. You must neither go off to the left or right, nor stay still like a corpse or a sack of rotting flesh.

But this does not mean that you should practice both things—movement and stillness—simultaneously. While you're in zazen, it's activity within stillness. However, when you take part in the ceremony, do *gassho* or *sampai*, it's stillness within activity. Don't do both at once. Zazen during zazen. *Samu* during *samu*. *Shikantaza*: just zazen; *shikansamu*: just *samu*.

One day Master Deshimaru said, "Even if you practice zazen until you die, if you do not practice it as I have taught you, it will not be *ku sokuze shiki, shiki sokuze ku.*" What he meant was, if you don't concentrate on the original, if you stagnate in duality, your practice will not be emptiness that becomes form and form that becomes emptiness. It will stay on one side: just form, just emptiness.

❦

Sometimes when he referred to this matter of concentration, Master Deshimaru spoke quite simply: "Sit on two chairs and you will fall down; love two women at once and you will not really have either of them."

This is fairly obvious. Dedicating yourself to two things is very difficult. Dedicating your life to the piano and to being a Zen monk, for example, is not so easy. Of course you can play the piano and be a Zen monk at the same time. But I'm talking about dedicating yourself to something entirely. I'm talking about the total commitment that makes zazen the absolute center of your life. If your career as a pianist takes the central place in your life, then it's hard to have zazen as the absolute center.

I think what you have to do, if you have two tendencies— which is the case for most of us, and I'm speaking from experience—is to find out how to unify them. You achieve this through the practice.

We could even say that two are really two only when they are One. True diversity, true difference, is found in oneness of mind, in the original.

❦

If you do not concentrate on the original,
The merits of both extremes will be lost.

How can we put Sosan's words into practice? How can we concentrate on this oneness of mind, this originality?

In order to do this, your energy must circulate freely. This energy is called *ki*. To practice the Way, you need powerful *ki*. And to create powerful *ki*, you must not follow your thoughts, not have obstacles or personal thoughts in your head. This is what is meant by "abandon everything," those words so often repeated in Zen. This is what all the great masters did, and it's what you should read between the lines of almost every strophe in the *Shinjinmei*, especially the early ones.

In an eighteenth-century manuscript on the art of *budo*,[10] there is much talk of *ki*. This manuscript describes how *ki* can be tied up by thinking. The author, martial arts master Chissai, explains how, in the art of *budo*, the person whose *ki* is hampered by overly yin thinking is slow to draw his sword—which is not a very good thing when facing an opponent who's hoping to cut off your head. But conversely, when *ki* overflows, when it's too intense or too yang, it breaks up into agitation and becomes superficial and inconsistent, making you like "dry leaves swept away by the wind."

We've all had this experience, in zazen, for example: when the mind has the right attitude, it circulates without obstruction, as opposed to the mind that stagnates, stuck on one thought or another. This mind activity has no beginning and no end, like a river. It is continuous and unique. No simpler movement exists, and it is through this movement that *ki* is developed.

The *ki* in question here is *joriki*. *Jo* means "the energy which comes from the *hara*"; *riki* means "solidity," "strength." *Joriki* describes the energy produced by zazen.

Chissai also tells us that heart and *ki* are basically one. And in order for *ki* to be exact, authentic, unconscious, natural and automatic, a transparent heart is necessary, a heart which nothing comes to darken.

Zazen is heart. Zazen is direct communication, person to person, heart to heart, without anything coming in between. Body and mind can thus become a channel through which cosmic *ki* circulates—*ki* which is then no different from *hannya*, wisdom.

[10] The *Tengugeijutsuron* (1730).

69

Master Deshimaru once said that *ki* was the mind's ability to react to a spiritual impetus. It's the *ki* we need to seek out the spiritual path and stay there. It's a spiritual impulse that we've all felt many times; otherwise we would never have discovered zazen.

This spiritual impulse, this pure *ki*, is, quite simply, faith. Not faith in the Christian sense of faith in God, which is separation; but faith in the sense of faith without object, which is non-separation.

Many people do *gassho* to the statue of Buddha on the altar; some bow to the master's portrait. But the statue is just a piece of wood or metal, the portrait is just a photo. *Gassho* is a more profound gesture than that, a gesture directed towards the human heart—which is also the animal heart, and the God heart as well.

The faith I'm talking about is what the masters call "fundamental cosmic energy" or "original mind." So when you want to concentrate on original mind, you must be completely sincere . . . which is not easy.

You may have heard the story of the Tibetans Milarepa and Marpa. Milarepa left Marpa, his guru (that's the term he himself used) to follow someone else. At the time, he didn't have total faith in Marpa and, with the help of Marpa's wife, he stole some documents, various relics, books and images. Then he went to the new guru saying, "Here are some gifts from Marpa, who has given me permission to practice with you."

The new guru accepted Milarepa because of the documents and gifts which Marpa was supposed to have given him. But he very quickly realized that something wasn't quite right with this new disciple. Milarepa was not progressing in the practice. The new guru realized that there was no reason to go on this way and sent Milarepa back to Marpa.

The meaning of this story is that in the end, when you want to concentrate on true originality—or oneness of mind, or the unique Way—authentic faith is indispensable. And when you lie, cheat or steal, true faith does not exist. The story of Milarepa has therefore to do with true faith, the faith that goes further than God and Buddha, even beyond the words "God" and "Buddha."

Faith is the intuition that the truth is present in this very moment. Faith is knowing this—and not through rational thought, but in your marrow, in your blood. Faith is what is lived, what is experienced, what is understood. It is the true understanding which is not found in words, and not the comparative or erroneous understanding that most people have.

> *If you do not concentrate on the original,*
> *The merits of both extremes will be lost.*

And so, concentrate on the origin; that's where true understanding is, where true faith is, where true tranquility is.

❦

At the end of a sesshin, everyone can see that postures and minds have changed. Everyone becomes calm, everyone returns to the normal condition, to what I would call the true tranquility of our fundamental nature.

Original nature, *the original* that Sosan is referring to in the thirteenth strophe of the *Shinjinmei*, is complete tranquility.

I'm not talking about the tranquility that we all experience from time to time, when we close the door and feel happy to be home again, alone or with family. That tranquility is short-lived, limited and isolated, and it often shatters as soon as we go out into the world and come up against annoyance, deception and failure. No, here I'm talking about true, unconditional and irreversible tranquility, the kind that a person who is *mushin*—no-mind— feels every day, alone or with others.

Tranquility or original nature, the true self, has nothing to do with the Christian belief that true tranquility is found in God. For Buddhists, it's not a question of God, but of Self. And people who practice zazen know that they are not separate from Buddha; they seek Buddha within themselves.

This being so, we always come back to the same question: What is mind? Master Dogen says he has no idea…. Just observe the dew on the grass. Maybe we can say that mind is complete tranquility. Words are never adequate to describe original nature.

How do we obtain what Sosan calls *the merits of both extremes*? Unconsciously and automatically.

Remember the story of Raisan, the master who farted? He was so concentrated on his sweet potato that he completely ignored the imperial messenger and didn't even stop to wipe his nose. Concentrating on the little details, concentrating on the big ones—it's the same thing. And Raisan's seeing no reason to wipe his nose is like Hojo's saying, "Mind itself is Buddha." No opposition, no separation. If concentration is natural and unconscious, the merits of both extremes will not be lost.

Zazen is natural and unconscious concentration on the original, on One. That's why you should continue zazen—I mean zazen mind—all the time, outside the dojo as well as inside.

All those who have practiced and eventually find themselves confronted with death surely ask themselves, "What was important in my life?" and "What will make me more peaceful when it's time to die?" At that moment, they surely remember zazen: "During zazen, I used my time fully and totally. All the other time—time for work, time for love, time for eating, time for drinking—wasn't really so important."

And why would you think of zazen when you're about to die? Because zazen mind never dies.

14

If you accept only one existence, you will fall into that single existence.
If you become attached to ku, you will turn yourself against it.

This means that if you stick to *shiki* (phenomena), you'll end up being trapped by them. But if you run exclusively after *ku* (vacuity, solitude, spirituality), you'll become its enemy.

In this strophe, Sosan explains that we must not fall into one of these categories, *shiki* or *ku*, at the exclusion of the other. But this also means that we should not confuse one of these options with reality. We shouldn't get stuck on words. All the misery on this earth comes from words.

You have to study Zen writings to understand *ku*: the emptiness from which all things come, the mind, inseparable from *shiki*, phenomena. Every time Master Deshimaru talked about *ku*, he talked about *shiki*. *Ku sokuze shiki*: emptiness becomes phenomena; and vice versa: *shiki sokuze ku*.

And so this strophe talks about *shiki sokuze ku*: the phenomena that become non-phenomena. *Shiki sokuze ku*, but also, *ku sokuze shiki*. Don't dwell on phenomena or non-phenomena.

If *ku* is seen as the opposite of existence—in other words, phenomena—it is no longer true *ku*. In the same way, if existence is opposed to *ku*, it is no longer true existence. If light were only light, it would not be light.

The *Sandokai*, composed by Master Sekito, contains this very famous verse, which evokes the same principle:

> *Darkness exists within light,*
> *Light exists within darkness.*

This expresses the non-duality of things. Form and non-form, material and spiritual, visible and invisible . . . one which is also the other.

That's why following *ku* is actually going against it. *Ku*: in Sanskrit, *sunyata*. For lack of a better word, it is usually translated as "vacuity." But *ku* is not, for example, the emptiness of a hole. There's no inside or outside. Master Deshimaru used to say that *ku* can be seen as God or Buddha, though it is not a God outside of us.

Tanka was a monk, a disciple of Sekito. Once he spent the night in a temple near Peking. It was very cold and he found himself alone in the buddha-hall with three wooden Buddha statues. Tanka took one and burned it to warm himself. Smelling smoke, the abbot—who had a handsome white beard and bushy eyebrows—came running. He was shocked.

"What have you done? You've burned the Buddha statue!"

Tanka took a stick and poked in the ashes.

The abbot, taken aback, tugged at his beard and asked, "What are you looking for?"

"I'm looking for the Buddha's *sarira*." (*Sarira* are the remains of a saint's cremation.)

"You're crazy!" said the abbot. "How can you find the *sarira* of a wooden statue?"

Tanka, who was still freezing, replied, "In that case, what if we burn the other two?"

The abbot thought the monk was dangerous and insane, and he threw him out into the icy cold. The next morning, when the abbot got up and went out to see what had happened to the crazy monk, he saw Tanka doing *gassho* to a boundary stone.

"What are you doing?" asked the abbot.

Tanka was reciting a mantra for the Buddha, the Dharma, the Sangha and all sentient beings. But the abbot didn't understand.

"I don't need your statues to do *gassho*," Tanka told him. "I create Buddha wherever I am."

Shortly after this incident, the abbot lost his white beard and eyebrows, which is a sign of spiritual retribution. The abbot, who had held on to *ku* and had held on to *shiki*, didn't even have a beard to hold on to anymore.

৵৵

It is true that the phenomenal world exists. Buddha himself said so. But everything that exists as phenomena exists only through conditions, causes and effects. In other words, phenomena exist, but they have no noumenon, no eternal substance. And *ku* has no noumenon either.

There are some people who think that everything is illusion. But if you think that way, you forget that everything is mind. We say, "no substance, no noumenon," but we should also say that everything is noumenon. Noumenon can be God or Buddha. Hindus worship a river, the Ganges. Buddhists venerate a tree, the *bodhi* tree. So where is emptiness?

Gensha was a disciple of Seppo. Tired of hearing Seppo say the same thing all the time, one day he told himself, "I'm going to go see another master." And he left. While walking in the mountains, he badly stubbed his big toe. Suddenly he said, "The body does not exist. Where does this pain come from?" And exactly at that moment, Gensha had a great satori. Without hesitating, he went back to see Seppo: no need to change masters.

Existence without noumenon, *ku*, becomes existence. When this realization comes from the body rather than from the head or philosophical discourse or books, then this awakening, this satori, is irreversible.

ক৯

From the moment you try to express the non-duality of things, One appears. And in fact this strophe also talks about One.

One day, Tozan decided to leave his master, Ungan. Ungan was dying, and Tozan didn't stay behind to hold his hand. But they did have this mondo:
"After your death, Master, if I am asked what your true face was, what should I answer?"
"*Tada kore kore*. Only this is this."
Tozan went away not understanding, and this answer has remained a very famous koan.
Often, when One is referred to, it becomes a koan, or rather the reference is expressed in the form of a koan—in other words, something you can't understand rationally with your frontal brain or with an academic or scientific mind. Tozan didn't understand, even though he had the *shiho*, his master's certification. (The *shiho* means you understand what you understand, that you've really assimilated the teaching and the practice.)
And so Tozan had just left his master. He was all alone. He had been walking for a few days when he crossed a bridge. He glanced at the water

flowing below and saw his face. At that moment, Tozan understood his master's last words, "Only this is this." And he composed this poem:

In the mirror of the water, my image and its reflection face each other. My body, my shape, is not my reflection, but the reflection is me.

∽❦∽

Don't fall into the situation described in the fourteenth strophe; don't dwell on a single existence.

Here again we touch on the question of faith. Not dualistic faith between God and me, but, as Dogen explained it, faith which is whole, a body.

It may be hard to understand, but it's even harder to express. It is beyond words. Here's an image: a fish swimming in the water. The water is one with the fish. One cannot exist without the other. And so the fish is the water, and the water is the fish. This is the body of faith.

No separation. If you can live this in your guts, in and through your body, you will be deeply tranquil, even in the midst of conflict. Even if you find yourself in hell, inner tranquility will be there.

15

Even if your words are correct, even if your thoughts are exact,
It is not in accordance with the truth.

It follows that Master Sosan himself, in composing the *Shinjinmei*, was not in accordance with the truth. And so, even if everything is correct in this poem, even if there is not the slightest error, this is not in accordance with the truth—and in the same way, neither are my commentaries on it.

In Strophes 15 and 16, Sosan tells us that Zen—zazen—cannot be explained in words. In the *Rules for Kosho Ji*, Master Dogen said that books about Zen are unnecessary: you can read all the correct, exact writing on Zen that you like, but it's still not in accordance with the truth.

In terms of the fifteenth strophe, Master Deshimaru said, "Zen should not talk too much or think too much…. Reading ten thousand sutras, ten thousand books, is completely useless."

This is why *doshu* is very important: how you express the Way. If you think too much, if you talk too much, this does not conform to the behavior of a person of the Way. And the opposite is no better. In fact, in Zen, we have transmission from mind to mind, from heart to heart: *i shin den shin*.

At the beginning of sesshin, I often say that we must be concentrated on all our actions and all our behavior. Each of us expresses the Way personally, subjectively, through our body, in zazen, in *kinhin*, in *samu*, in bed, in the way we sleep, the way we wake up, during meals, in silence, by the way we chant the meal sutra.

Here's the story of Tokujo, the master who became a ferryman, and his disciple, the monk Kassan. One day, they had a mondo on a boat. Kassan spoke well; Tokujo threw him in the water. This happened several times, and each time that Kassan found himself in the water, Tokujo hit him on the head with a pole, saying, "Your answers, even if they are exact, are not correct!" It was like beating farts out of a dead donkey.

So the truth cannot be captured by words.

❦

What is in accordance with the truth? Maybe faith, because I think truth is simply the present moment. And since faith is also the present moment, it is in accordance with the truth.

To better understand this question of faith, it may be useful to understand the power and subtlety of the subconscious.

In a lecture about sutras, a contemporary Swiss Zen master, Michel Bovay, said, "If we are beyond words, we can understand words," adding that it's not necessary to recite the *Hannya Shingyo* in our native language, or to understand it consciously, even though it is written in Kanbun, a mixture of ancient Chinese and Sanskrit. It's the same thing for this phrase, taken from the four vows of the bodhisattva, chanted every day in Zen temples: *Shu jo muhen seigan do*, which means, "However numerous living beings, I vow to save them all." It's not necessary to translate it from the Japanese; simply chanting with a unified mind, being completely present, without understanding with your brain— that's saving all beings. You could even say that simply thinking the sutras, beyond words, without thinking, can influence all beings on this earth.

Your subconscious is enough. It influences your consciousness. Your *mushotoku* subconscious understands Kanbun very well, and the French or English translation doesn't interest the *mushotoku* subconscious. The subconscious is not limited by language.

One day, during a mondo, a young American asked me this question: "What can I do to help my family? Everyone around me is suffering, sick or dying."

"Chant a mantra," I replied.

"Oh no!" he cried. "I can't do that in front of my family!"

"You don't have to recite the words," I told him. "Breathe. That's enough."

Hannyatara was the master of Bodhidharma, who was the son of a king from southern India. One day, Hannyatara was invited to eat with the king.

"Please, Master, chant us a sutra before the meal."

There was a long silence.

"Okay, it's over."

"How is that possible?"

"Every time I inhale, I recite ten thousand sutras; every time I exhale, I recite another ten thousand."

The king was happy.

This is what abandoning language means. And this brings us directly to Strophe 16.

16

Abandoning language and thought
Will lead you beyond all places.

Abandoning language doesn't mean not talking anymore, just as abandoning thinking doesn't mean not thinking anymore.

Today, many people think there should be no oral teaching given during zazen. Several years ago in Paris, a disciple rather aggressively insisted that in ancient times, masters did not talk during zazen. He was supported by a fellow practitioner, who assured me that in ancient Chinese and Japanese monasteries, disciples didn't utter a word during the three months of summer camp.

Here's what Master Dogen said during one of the ninety-day summer retreats that he led with one or two of his disciples: "People today say that the ultimate truth cannot be explained in words. Words, they say, put us on the wrong track.... People today think that monks should remain completely apart from other people. [This means not only being isolated from the common world, but also keeping silent.] Who says that this ninety-day retreat is a wordless proclamation? Please, show me a true retreat led by Shakyamuni Buddha which was speechless."

Japanese philosophy professor and Zen monk Kazuo Morimoto sent one of my co-disciples an article he had written on the great philosopher Derrida's essay, *"Comment ne pas parler"* ("How to Not Talk").

My friend said to me, laughing, "Can you believe that? A whole piece on how not to talk!"

Then he admitted, "I didn't understand a word of it."

I said to him, "Give it to me. I'll understand it."

I read it. I didn't understand a word of it either. It was very complex. Morimoto seemed to be more professor than monk. But the article's conclusion was much easier to understand: "Derrida is seeking to shed light on the fact that, in the end, we cannot avoid speaking." The last sentence of the article was more interesting and profound: "The real world, without beginning or end, never stops talking about Itself."

Today there are Zen practices which allow no talking whatsoever. But that's not Zen; Zen uses everything: words, shouts, gestures, silence, the *kyosaku*, the *rensaku*, whisky, meat, tofu. It's important not to entertain illusions about anything. No ideas at all. *Maku mozo.*

That's what's written on one of the *kyosakus* in the Paris Dojo. It means, "No illusions." The Chinese master Daikaku answered every question with, "*Maku mozo*"—like Gutei, who always answered by holding up his thumb.

Words are necessary; otherwise, there would be no reason for an oral teaching to exist. Language can illustrate, and Zen teaching often uses this technique. But you have to be very careful not to get attached to words, not to take them too literally.

The emperor liked his prime minister, whose name was Kiyu. Although Kiyu was a little uptight about the purity of speech, the emperor respected him. He performed his ministerial role perfectly and was completely honest. The emperor was elderly and did not want to continue leading his empire. He had a young fiancée and wanted to go off quietly somewhere with her. And so he thought that Kiyu might take the situation in hand. One day, he summoned him to the palace and told him:

"Kiyu, I have known you for a long time. You are very honest and very competent. You are even capable of leading a nation. Therefore, I am considering entrusting my empire to you."

"What? Entrust me with your empire?"

"Yes."

"Well I never!" He put his hands over his ears and said, "You hurt me with these words, Emperor! Your words have dirtied my ears!" And he headed straight for the river.

A farmer whom Kiyu knew well was passing by, bringing his cow to market. He got to the edge of the river and saw Kiyu washing out his ears in the water.

"What are you doing there? Why are you washing your ears?"

"Today, I am truly furious. It so happens the emperor wanted to make me his successor. He offered me his empire! My ears have been dirtied, and so I am washing them."

"Rats," said the farmer, "I wanted to let my cow drink from this clear water, and now you've gone and spoiled it!"

Don't be attached to words, any more than to signs or ideas. Words and ideas can imprison people like birds in a cage.

One day, one of Buddha's disciples asked him this question: "Why does an ignorant person make discriminations while a wise person does not?"

Buddha replied, "Because the ignorant person is attached to names, signs and ideas."

For example, the ignorant person thinks that hell is a place where you're punished, and that nirvana is a place where you're blessed. The awakened person understands that these are just states of awareness, manifestations of states of mind. Unfortunately, it's because of this lack of understanding that we witness so many atrocities in the world. People become fanatic about the words of Jesus, or the words of Mohammed. Ironically, if we took away the words of Jesus, I don't know what would be left of Christianity. But I do believe that if we took away the words of Buddha, Zen would still exist, exactly as it does now.

⌘

So abandoning language means being beyond words, beyond language itself, beyond all places. Speech/no-speech, thought/no-thought . . . don't stop there. Don't get stuck on anything, taking one side or the other—either words or silence. *Funi*, not-two.

> *Silent is the cherry blossom*
> *In this early April,*
> *Rose is the color of spring.*
> *Without thought,*
> *The music of the wind in the pines*
> *Plays its splendid melody.*

That's satori. It's like a fish swimming in water, or a bird flying in the sky.

Here's a poem by Master Dogen, translated by Master Deshimaru:

As the water is clear right through to the bottom,
The fish which swims realizes the fish itself.
As the sky is wide and spreads to infinity,
The bird which flies realizes the bird itself.

Master Deshimaru wrote this poem on the first rakusu he gave me, before my bodhisattva ordination. I had worked with him for hours to translate it from the Japanese, trying to understand what he wanted to express. Many other translations existed, but none of them satisfied him. Here, for example, is the translation of the second part of the poem, by Dutch-born artist and writer Frederick Franck:

I see the birds flying in the sky,
They fly on and on
Never reaching the boundary of the sky.

As if the sky had boundaries! That's what our practice is like—beyond all places.

17

If you return to the original root, you touch the essence.
If you follow enlightenment, you lose the original source.

When talking about the Way, Master Deshimaru often advised us to "look for the roots, not the leaves." But what is the root, the source? Where is it? Where is the source of a river? The source is in the current. By that I mean that the source is not just here, it is also now.

And what are the leaves? Satori. Nirvana. Awakening. Knowledge. Strophe 17 contains the kanji *sho*, which Master Deshimaru translated as "enlightenment," and also as "shining phenomenon." Those are the leaves. Follow them and you could wind up in a mental hospital. Once I read an article about people who went mad following satori. It was surely written from a Soto Zen standpoint. And in fact Master Deshimaru and Master Dogen are saying the same thing.

During sesshin, after ten days of intensive zazen, your mind becomes a little like a mirror in which *ku* is reflected, and *shiki* too, the "shining phenomenon." Yet this "shining phenomenon" has no influence, because it passes. Everything passes. When "it" passes, there's no more separation.

Before he became a master, Tokusan was a famous scholar. He had written twelve big volumes of commentaries on the *Diamond Sutra*, and was praised in academic circles and the court as the greatest scholar of his time. One day, he heard about a certain Zen master named Ryutan. Tokusan was intrigued and a little jealous. He decided to test this master, so he went off to see him, carrying all his sutra commentaries with him. On his way, he stopped to buy a rice cake from an old woman.

"Tell me, honorable monk, what's in that big bag?" asked the woman.

"In this bag, I have many volumes of commentaries on the *Diamond Sutra*. My name is Tokusan. Haven't you heard about me and my work?"

"No, afraid not," replied the old woman. "But I did hear the *Diamond Sutra* being recited once. Can I ask you a question about it?"

All Tokusan wanted was his rice cake, but he nodded and she continued.

"If you buy this rice cake, what mind will you eat it with?"

Tokusan stood with his mouth agape, unable to answer. He left without eating his rice cake. When he arrived at Ryutan's monastery, he was no longer so sure of himself and his knowledge as when he had set out. But now it was time to meet the master. He and Ryutan spoke late into the night. Finally the master said, "It's very late. Why don't you go to bed?"

When Tokusan stepped out of Ryutan's hut, he found himself in pitch darkness.

"I can't see a thing out here," he said.

"Take this," said Ryutan, offering Tokusan a candle. But just as he handed it to him, he blew out the flame. Tokusan had satori.

ॐ

So we must come back to the root. The root also means the root of our thoughts, which is *ku*. Our thinking comes from *ku*, and sometimes that thinking becomes action. But often, by the time we're into the action, we've forgotten the source.

People make decisions and don't remember them; they make promises to themselves, then forget them; they begin a job and pretty soon they don't know what made them get into it; they make a vow—*the* vow, *kan*—and little by little, they forget. They forget why they practice.

It's often said that you should forget, forget, forget. Dogen himself said it. But you shouldn't forget everything. The great vow is very important. Master Deshimaru used to say that all buddhas make this vow, and bodhisattvas too.

In the same way, you always hear "*mushotoku, mushotoku,* no goal"—but within *mushotoku*, there's *shotoku*, goal. Great goals do exist, not just little egotistical goals like, "I'm going to become a good person, I'll never be angry or jealous again." But goals like, "I'm going to save others from my anger, my judgment, my disappointment." But little by little you get distracted, you forget these great goals. You see a couple of trees and think that's the whole forest. You tell yourself you have to forget everything and just practice zazen with no goal, *mushotoku*.

And of course, that's true; but you also have to come back to your roots, the roots of your beginning. When we first came to the dojo, we all had a goal. If you practice the right way, this goal, perhaps ill-defined at first, will become more and more precise, more and more defined. Otherwise, how can you do it? How can you continue? *Kan*, the vow, the promise. I can't imagine for one minute that someone could practice zazen for a long time without having secretly made that vow. And that's something you should never forget.

18

If you are enlightened in all directions, even for an instant,
It is superior to ordinary ku.

Out of the seventy-three strophes of this long poem, the
eighteenth is one of the most complicated, and perhaps one of the
most difficult to understand, even for me, even for other disciples
who've been practicing a long time. That's Buddhism: in the end,
it can't be understood.

Unlike many other strophes in the *Shinjinmei*, in which Sosan
expresses himself in concrete terms, this strophe may seem somewhat abstract. It deals with *ku*, the void from which all things
come. There's no appropriate word for *ku* in English. Sources such
as the *Shambhala Dictionary of Buddhism and Zen*[11] translate it as
"emptiness." But that's not really correct, because emptiness
always carries a sense of "nothing" as opposed to "something,"
whereas *ku* includes everything, all phenomena (*shiki*), including
those of the mind. The void, the *ku* that I'm talking about, is *ku*
and *shiki* working together: *ku sokuze shiki*—non-form becomes
form; or, if you prefer, non-phenomenon becomes phenomenon;
or, even more simply, non-form *is* form, non-phenomenon *is* phenomenon. And of course vice-versa: form (phenomenon) is non-
form (non-phenomenon).

Everyone who has practiced zazen for a while knows this. But
people who don't practice have a very different idea of *ku*; for the
scholar who studies and comments on Buddhism, for example, *ku*
is something else. In general, these people are looking outward,
while people who practice correctly are looking inward. If you
only look outward, you see only external emptiness, and because
of this you can't see the source of things. It's like the scientist who
studies a chair's composition with a microscope, and in the end
discovers that there's nothing—no existence. This discovery can

---

[11] Ingrid Fischer-Schreiber, Franz-Karl Ehrhard and Michael S. Diener,
ed., *The Shambhala Dictionary of Buddhism and Zen*, trans. Michael H.
Kohn (Boston: Shambhala, 1991).

lead the thinker to adopt the exteriorized outlook of nihilism. But this is not Soto Zen teaching, nor is it Buddha's.

Here's what Master Deshimaru says in his commentary on Strophe 18: "If we look inside ourselves, into our minds, there is no longer *shiki* or *ku*; and all the speeches about *ku*, about Buddha, about the Dharma, the never-ending discussions about Buddhism, are totally ineffective. The issue in Buddhism is just returning to the original ego, the original mind, without discussion or language."

So as long as enlightenment is directed towards external things, you can't see the source of things, and you remain at the level of the "ordinary *ku*" that Master Sosan is talking about.

The Japanese kanji for this term is *zenku*, which Master Deshimaru defined as "pre-*ku*." After studying Master Deshimaru's commentaries, after countless discussions with my co-disciples, after reading comments by Ch'an master Sheng-yen, Master Genpo and Professor Suzuki, I have come to understand that ordinary *ku* can mean the *appearance* of *ku* or the *thought* of *ku*.

Ordinary *ku* is therefore external *ku*, outer emptiness, or, if you prefer, the emptiness of forms exterior to oneself. It is intellectual *ku* (we could say the mundane void), and not inner, authentic *ku*, the *ku* which really concerns us, the *ku* we should contemplate, the *ku* which includes all other *ku*, and the *ku* which, in the end, is us, since we are everything.

Here is Strophe 18 put another way: "If, for a brief instant, we look inward, then we go beyond the emptiness of the things of this world."

❧

If you lack adequate self-knowledge, you will understand only ordinary *ku* and not authentic *ku*. On the other hand, if you are *enlightened in all directions, even for an instant*, it is superior to every appearance of *ku*, every thought of *ku*.

If you are enlightened in all directions: in other words, inside as well as outside. In his commentary, Master Deshimaru says,

"You must not reduce your problems to ego, hate, love, ugliness, beauty, notions of big, small, dark, light.... You should not see them from the outside with a dualistic vision, but in all directions, within yourself."

And thanks to this inner vision—thanks to this authentic *ku*, which enables us to open our eyes to see directly what being is—the small self dissolves in an instant, and we can see being in its entirety; we can see it here and now, because it's the reality of the moment which is transmitted by authentic *ku*. But there is no other reality: we do not exist in the past, or in the future. And so, as Sosan puts it in the seventy-fourth strophe, one instant becomes ten thousand years.

This also means that the transmission from Buddha and Bodhidharma exists outside of time and space. In Zen practice, we have the essential expression *i shin den shin*: from heart-mind to heart-mind. Master Deshimaru used to say, "from my soul to your soul." And that's what has been transmitted down to our time. You can't get ordained by mail-order. Although you are given a kesa or rakusu at that moment, it's not the actual cloth that's being transmitted; although the *ketsumyaku* you receive at that moment is only paper, it is written in red, symbolizing blood and the body—in other words, from the inside, not from the outside.

True Buddhism did not begin with external things: special robes, or writing, or sutras; it began when man first looked inside himself. That was the beginning of the practice of the Way. And with the arrival of Bodhidharma in China sometime in the fifth or sixth century, this inner regard began to develop through a physical, human practice—body to body, body-mind to body-mind.

19

Change in ordinary ku
Requires the birth of illusions.

Ordinary *ku* is *ku* that is exterior to us, false *ku*—false because it is dependent on the changing conceptions created by our personal consciousness. Thus, *change in ordinary ku requires the birth of illusions* means that ordinary *ku* is a *ku* that depends on our illusions, in other words, on language and thought.

Whether we use English, French or Hindi, as soon as we start talking about *ku*, it becomes ordinary *ku*. Same thing if we say or think *ku*: it becomes illusion. Why? Because our personal consciousness is once again creating categories.

It's like wanting to think *hishiryo*. *Hi* is "beyond" and *shiryo* is "thinking." When you try to do it deliberately, "thinking beyond thinking" becomes an ordinary, even speculative thought.

Once, during a summer retreat with Master Deshimaru, a professor came up to me and said, "I understand everything the master is saying. *Ku, mushotoku*—it's easy. But I haven't got *hishiryo* yet. Could you please explain it to me?"

Impossible. All explanations are necessarily limited to the domain of concepts, which are of course changeable, since they are created by us—by our small minds.

༄

Change in ordinary ku
Requires the birth of illusions.

I think this strophe means that all change, all personal coming-and-going, all our stories of love or failure in love, everything we think is real and that we get attached to—all of that requires the birth of illusions.

In the Zen world, it's fairly common for disciples to want to get out of their attachment to existence—which they put in the same category as visible phenomena—and move towards the idea of non-existence. But being attached to this supposed non-existence, this *ku*, and telling yourself, "that's where true wisdom is," is also ordinary, false *ku*. Ordinary *ku*, then, would be only the appearance of *ku*, the idea we form of it. And according to Strophe 19, we would get stuck in this appearance.

From 1971 to 1982, Master Deshimaru taught every day at a Zen dojo on the rue Pernety in Paris's 14th *arrondissement*. One day as I was leaving the dojo, I met a Rinzai monk. I didn't know he was Rinzai, but he was very impressive-looking—big and strong, his face clear and direct. He wore the full monk's habit—black kolomo, white kimono—and other things too, belts and sashes. I can still see Master Deshimaru coming out of the dojo and catching sight of this monk. His reaction was completely different from mine. He looked at the monk severely and made him come to his room. I saw that he wasn't pleased, but I didn't really understand what was going on.

The next day, Master Deshimaru talked about this monk in the kusen, saying that he had understood nothing about Buddhism, never mind Zen. Then he spoke directly to us in these terms:

"You must have confidence in yourselves and not only follow form. You must understand more deeply than other monks. You must not make mistakes. If someone wears a monk's robe, you should not make assumptions based on his appearance. If someone lives in a monastery, you should not follow him in his error, influenced by the size of the monastery."

This Rinzai monk, all decked out in a special kolomo, with a special belt and sandals, certainly seemed to proclaim authentic *ku*. But in Master Deshimaru's view, there was nothing authentic about it. Master Deshimaru never put stock in appearance or age or clothes, but in what is invisible, ageless and permanent. For him, all the rest was just illusion.

All the masters tell us that we shouldn't be taken in by the appearance of things. So don't rely on images, even subtle ones; otherwise you'll think they coincide with the objects you're trying to represent. But an image is only an image, and in the end it represents nothing—nothing but ordinary *ku*. It can't capture Buddha-nature, which is in each of us, and which has no image or face.

Maybe that's why Soto Zen attaches no importance to images or statues, such as a Buddha statue on an altar. Just as Buddha asked his disciples not to worship his person, so we do not worship Buddha or the master. When we do *gassho* towards the altar when entering and leaving the dojo, it's not for the statue of Buddha, or for the photos of the master. So what are we doing *gassho* to? We do *gassho* to what is highest in us, that is, the human heart.

∾

In his commentary on Strophe 19, Master Deshimaru wanted to show the difference between ordinary *ku* and authentic *ku*, or impermanent *ku* and permanent *ku*—a difference which the strophe itself does not entirely elucidate. To illustrate this, he compared Hinayana consciousness—that of the Small Vehicle, which adheres above all to following the rules and precepts—and Mahayana consciousness—that of the Great Vehicle, which does not confine itself to the precepts and sutras, to speeches and lectures, but extends to Buddha-nature, which is unlimited, infinite and inexplicable.

Using this comparison, he spoke about the difference between what is relative, changeable, based on a viewpoint connected to specific places, customs, political circumstances and time periods; and what has been perpetuated until now without change—the authentic essence which has survived to this day.

The difference between ordinary *ku* and authentic *ku* is like this. Times change constantly, as does the surface of Buddhism. Take for example the attitude towards women in the sangha. In the ancient times of primitive Buddhism, this attitude was completely different from what it is today. "Now that women have [the right to enter the homeless life]," said Shakyamuni Buddha, "the holy life will not last long, the true Dharma will last for only five hundred years."[12] These ideas, which may seem shocking today, were formed in a particular context and related to the moral constraints of the period. It should be noted, however, that despite Buddha's reluctance to accept women into the sangha, he

---

[12] H.W. Schumann, *The Historical Buddha* (London: Penguin/Arkana, 1989), p. 117.

was nonetheless one of the very first spiritual leaders to do so. After his death, women were in fact quickly excluded again. Over the centuries, they have been by turns admitted and rejected.

And so if authentic *ku*, this essence I'm talking about, keeps the image or tone of ancient times, or the morality of past eras, it's only ordinary *ku*, it's only the surface of things. It has nothing to do with the authentic mind which has come to us without change.

∽

If Master Deshimaru established a parallel between ordinary *ku* and Hinayana, it's because Hinayana Buddhism holds to the idea that we must do precisely what is said in the sutras.

I think that when it gets stuck on the words pronounced by Buddha 2,500 years ago, Hinayana Buddhism is not taking into account the fact that life in India at that time was very different, and that the first rules, the precepts, were adapted to the mentality of the people of that precise time period and that particular continent.

In Buddha's time, people lived outdoors, survived by begging, and did many other things which are no longer done today, such as contemplating corpses in cemeteries. The monks of Buddha's sangha were very rude, primitive in their manners, and even obtuse. They had to be educated, which is why rules were established which were much stricter than those of today. Beside the fact that Buddha was not exactly satisfied with their behavior, he also had to take into account the reaction of the villagers, who called the monks sitting in zazen "dumb pigs." So he told his disciples that when they assembled, they should recite the rules he had formulated for them. That's what they did, and it greatly impressed people—more than seeing the monks sitting in zazen. The rules forbidding the consumption of alcohol, for example, were established because one or two monks were found dead-drunk in the village. But it's ridiculous to take that and proclaim today, "You shouldn't drink alcohol! Buddha said so!"

Here's an image from the *Shobogenzo*: a samurai on a boat inadvertently drops his sword into the water. He immediately takes out a knife and marks, on the edge of the boat, the exact spot where the sword fell, so he can find it again later on.

This is a metaphor for ordinary *ku*. When the samurai marks the edge of the boat to show the spot where he should be able to find the sword, it's his personal consciousness acting, which doesn't take into account the passing of time, the water, the ever-changing river. Looking for a sword in water using a mark made on the edge of a boat is the same thing as saying, "Buddha said it 2,500 years ago, so it's the truth." It's impermanent, ordinary *ku*.

If it's not experienced personally, if it's not lived firsthand, then it's not the zazen of the present moment.

Many current masters, even Zen masters, follow the sutras to the letter: "Buddha said this, so we must do it." They say they practice the pure teaching of Buddha. They recommend, for example, abstaining from alcohol and cigarettes. And monks are totally celibate, otherwise they're excommunicated. They also conduct prolonged fasts, and when they allow themselves to eat, it's always vegetarian, also on pain of severe reprisal and, in some cases, excommunication.

Near the end of the last decade, the International Zen Association received a letter from a disciple of a very famous Zen master. It was a "message for the new century." It told us that we should abandon drinking and smoking and learn to live simply in our daily lives; this way, we could heal and fulfill our ideal of compassion. To this end, the disciples of the Zen master in question were contacting us to ask us to commit to not drinking alcohol, especially during retreats.

In our sangha, we don't allow any alcohol during sesshin, and outside of that, you shouldn't drink too much anyway; do as Dogen says in the *Fukanzazengi*: "Eat and drink simply. Reject all commitments and abandon all business. Do not think, 'this is good, this is bad.' Do not take sides for or against."

During a recent summer retreat at La Gendronnière Temple, a young practitioner asked me if I could make a separate table for vegetarians, since "people were fed up with always eating meat."

"Always eating meat?" I replied. "But there wasn't any last night."

"What do you mean there wasn't any!"
He had found a tiny piece of ham in his soup.

None of this has any importance. It's the inside you have to develop and deepen, not the surface of things, the ordinary *ku*; it's the inner resolution we have made in secret, the *kan*. *Kan* means not getting stuck on a piece of ham. This way you can live authentic *ku*, the essence. This essence came through Bodhidharma, passed through Eka, Sosan, Eno, Nyojo, Dogen, Keizan, Kodo Sawaki, Taisen Deshimaru and his disciples, and has come to us today—this essence which is nothing other than Buddha-nature.

And this transmission of Buddha-nature, which is not ordinary *ku*, this essence directly lived by Bodhidharma, did not stay locked up in India, as Hinayana asserts; it did not remain fixed in time; it was not content simply to go from Kapila, Buddha's birthplace, to Kuchira, where he died. On the contrary, it went through all the patriarchs, all the changes of time, all the changes of place, without changing one iota.

By comparing Hinayana and Mahayana, I think Master Deshimaru wanted to show that Mahayana—that is, Bodhidharma sitting with no goal—perpetuates Buddha-awareness with exactitude. It's the experience that we have in the here and now. Mahayana, as opposed to Hinayana, is therefore the direct realization of the Buddha-nature which Bodhidharma speaks about, a realization which is inexplicable and which does not depend on the birth of illusions or on changeable concepts created by our personal consciousness.

Only that which is ordinary can be explained; the essence of things—unlimited and infinite Buddha-nature—is inexplicable.

20

Do not seek the truth;
Simply be free from prejudice.

You might consider this strophe as a mantra to protect your mind. And if you do what it says—if you don't seek the truth and you stay free of prejudice—you're protecting not only your own mind, but everyone else's as well.

Anyone who has practiced zazen for two or three years or who has received the monk's or nun's ordination knows this. It's not hard to understand: we should stop seeking the truth; otherwise, we're heading straight for a dead end. And we also know perfectly well that prejudice is not a good thing.

But even people who have been ordained for twenty, thirty, forty or a hundred years do not always know how to put these instructions into practice. For example, you often hear, "Don't run after anything." But once again, it's easy to say, and suddenly to stop running after things is not the answer.

Generally, in life, you run after illusions like happiness and success. You run after phenomena, *shiki.* You run after women, you run after men. You run after sex, love, family, money, power. And if you don't run after illusions, you run after what you think is the truth. If you're not chasing women, you're chasing *mu*—nothing. It's the same thing.

In Zen, we like *mu* and we run after it in one way or another. You do zazen and use it as a method or a means not to run after illusions. You observe and observe and observe yourself. But if you can't manage to really forget yourself, then you fall into the opposite trap. You say to yourself, "Now I understand: nothing exists. *Mu.* I'm like Buddha: *mu.* When I do zazen, I'm in absolute, true reality."

So the master asks his disciple, "How's it going? How are you feeling today?"

Disciple: "I'm fine. I'm nothing."

Master: "Oh yeah? Nothing?"

Disciple: "Yep. Nothing. What do you think, Master?"

Master: "Drop all that nonsense!"

Disciple: "How can you ask me to drop 'that nonsense' when I just told you I already have?"

Master: "Well in that case, you still have to throw it away."

Neither seek the truth nor flee from illusions, because from a higher point of view, even the truth is prejudice and illusion.

The masters of the transmission insist on telling us that existence is only a phenomenon that comes from the cosmic system, and that truth and illusion are just two shadows in a mirror. And these two shadows, the shadow of truth and the shadow of illusion, come from our personal consciousness. Your desire becomes a vision—my desire, my vision, my shadow....

The master probably wants us to be neither with *mu* nor without *shiki*. He wants us to understand that thoughts in themselves are not a burden; but running after them, or running away from them, even a little bit, becomes a big burden, which completely obscures the practice of the Way.

To seek the truth, you have to go from thought to thought; and going from thought to thought—to use an image from ancient Zen—is like leaving your house and going where the grass grows, the grass of your thoughts. Zen masters are always telling us to let our thoughts pass. It may be the expression Master Deshimaru repeated most often in the fifteen years he spent in Europe. And masters from a thousand years ago were saying the same thing, always the same thing: "Don't complicate your life, go directly to the source." At that time, they often used the terms "east, west, north and south." Master Tozan said, "You must go neither west nor east, but rather head straight towards the place where, for ten thousand miles, not a single blade of grass exists." "Go neither west nor east" means we should abandon ourselves, and our awareness, which is steeped in prejudice.

In Strophe 59 of the *Shinjinmei*, Sosan refers to *hishiryo*. It's the first time in the history of Zen that this word appears. *Hishiryo* means thinking not-thinking/not-thinking thinking. If you do this, says Sosan, your mind won't even have time to create prejudice.

People who live at La Gendronnière Temple say, "Come to La Gendronnière, it's better than Paris, it's better than Berlin, better than Amsterdam!" Well, that's not true. Other people say the opposite: "Paris is better than La Gendronnière. There are more activities, a lot of lectures on Buddhism. The traffic jams and pollution aren't bad; they make us stronger!" This is also not true. Some people are looking for heat and go the tropics; others are looking for cold and go to the North Pole. They say the heat, or the cold, is good; or the opposite—they want to avoid one or the other.

One day, a disciple asked the master, "When it's cold or hot, what should I do to avoid the cold or the heat?"

The master replied, "Why don't you go where it is neither cold nor hot?"

At this point, the disciple could have had satori, but such was not the case, and the disciple insisted.

"Where is this place that is neither cold nor hot?"

The master replied, "In winter, let the cold kill you. In summer, let the heat kill you."

That's what not seeking the truth and not being prejudiced means. No need to escape the heat, no need to escape the cold; no need to escape unhappiness to look for happiness. It's *sandokai*: *san*, "difference"; *do*, "equality"; *kai*, "meeting" or "conjunction." It's being intimate with everything. And we cannot teach, we cannot give or receive, if we are not capable of becoming intimate with everything, including pain and suffering. That's the beginning of the practice and the source of compassion.

Zen teaching, the practice of zazen, is the greatest intimacy that exists.

But you won't find this intimacy if you're looking outward (and we're almost always looking outward), because then the light emanating from you is focused exclusively on your personal desires. In the end, the house is dark.

So the sage, who doesn't run away from or chase after anything, is always trying to change people's awareness, their way of seeing things. He says, "Turn this light inward, naturally." And, if people are listening, and are willing to practice, their minds turn around, completely and effortlessly. Because although it may require practice, looking inward with your mind requires no effort at all; it's not like turning a crank or climbing a pole using your muscles.

One single look: Gutei's thumb.

❧

"Be in harmony with the cosmos," Master Deshimaru often said. "Being in harmony with the cosmic system is true wisdom," he says in his commentary on Strophe 20. But egoism and individualism are obstacles to this harmony, this wisdom, this satori, because it's the small mind that runs after the truth, not the cosmic mind, not the great mind that Sosan is talking about and in which you must have faith. That mind never runs after anything.

Neither for nor against. Like nature: *inmo*—just this. That's true wisdom, true freedom.

Simply be free in the present moment, in other words not attached to what's happening here and now, what's happening within change. And everything is change.

As soon as you're free within impermanence, as soon as you become intimate with *mujo*, you're practicing the Way of the masters and patriarchs.

In the dojo at La Gendronnière Temple, there's a wind-bell hanging from the beam just next to the master's seat; it's called a *furin*. Master Nyojo, Dogen's master, wrote a poem on this subject:

> *The furin hangs in the sky, in the cosmos;*
> *It is free.*
> *When the wind comes from the East—*
> *Okay, it rings, ding, ding, ding…*
> *When the wind comes from the West—*
> *Okay, it rings, ding, ding, ding…*

It's another way of saying:

> *Do not seek the truth;*
> *Simply be free from prejudice.*

Do not dwell on opposites.
Do not seek out dualism.

This strophe warns us against getting stuck on a relative viewpoint. No duality, no preferences. That's a leitmotif in Zen. You find it everywhere, in all the poems, all the writings.

Buddha, Zen…it's all very simple. But lapse into dualism, lean to one side or the other, and Buddhism disappears. So keep away from ideas of left, right, correct, incorrect, good, bad, me, you. Don't run after the truth; don't be attached to One, don't be attached to Buddha-mind, to zazen, or to the posture. I remember one elder disciple of Master Deshimaru's who was always saying, "It's the posture that interests me. I only feel good when I'm in the posture. All the rest is of no concern to me." This woman is no longer practicing today.

Running after the posture is no different than trying to get away from noise—that, too, is a preference. "Shunning noise," said Obaku one day, "is like throwing out the flour when making bread." True silence has nothing to do with the idea of escaping noise. True silence is when your thoughts go away—because thoughts are not quiet. Most of the time, even if you're not talking, even if your jaw's not moving, the words keep coming.

Here's a poem by Master Deshimaru:

In silence, immortal silence swells.
Joy comes without speaking.

❧

Do not seek out dualism.

Historically, there's been a lot of talk about duality. Shankara, a great eighth-century Hindu master, founded the School of Non-Dualism. Its philosophy stated that only One exists. Other schools supported the theory of pure dualism, saying that One cannot exist without Other, that a river needs two banks, that a baby needs a man and a woman in order to be conceived.

Today, we see everything through the prism of dualism: good, evil, right, wrong, object, subject…. For the ordinary mind in the ordinary world, this kind of dualistic thinking can be necessary. I was once asked if observing was a dualistic act: isn't observing necessarily observing someone or something else? It depends.

Early on in my Zen practice, I invited a friend to come to the Pernety Dojo in Paris. She was a psychologist—very curious, very intellectual. At the time, very little was known about Zen and zazen in Europe, and psychologists were somewhat suspicious. When she came, I was *kyosaku*, which meant I sat facing the others and got up to correct people's postures. So I saw that it was very hard for this woman to keep looking inward during zazen. She wanted to see what the other people were doing. She was sitting facing a window and was looking at the other people in the reflection in the glass, to be able to come away with a few images or memories. And during the mondo, she looked at the person asking the question, she looked at the master, she looked at the other people's faces, she studied their reactions. She was trying to figure out if she had gotten mixed up in a cult, if we weren't all a little nuts.

Some people practice subject-object duality, in which observing is a completely dualistic act. But for the person who has deeply integrated the practice into his or her life, observing is not necessarily a dualistic act. Observing is just observing. The person who observes is just observing, the person who hears is just hearing. The observer is *ku*. *Ku* is also the Way, the cosmic truth. From this non-dualistic state of mind, true creativity and humor can spring forth naturally. With non-duality, your mind becomes quick, keen, and at the same time, calm.

I've seen a number of social activists come through the dojo, people who want to save the world. They usually get frustrated with zazen. They say at least they're doing something, instead of sitting around facing the wall. Unfortunately, some people who work for the betterment of the world are completely sick themselves. And that's no way to help. It's better to adopt a non-dualistic outlook: by helping even just one person, even myself, I'm taking care of life in its totality. Because one person is all people.

This goes back to the Buddhist idea of *bodaishin*, Buddha-mind. It's not an individual mind, but the universal mind. Buddha-mind penetrates you and me—it's *ho ten*, the Dharma changing me, as opposed to *ga ten*, my ego changing the Dharma. It's like wearing the kesa. The Dharma is the Buddha-mind that changes me, changes you, changes us, changes the whole world.

In Zen, to talk about this mind, we have the metaphor of the moon reflected in water. The moon shines on the water of the lake, the wind blows in the pines. A poem from the *Sanshodoei* by Master Dogen says,

> *Without muddiness*
> *In the water of the mind,*
> *Clear is the moon.*
> *Even the waves break against it*
> *And are changed into light.*

Observing is just observing. If you just observe, just listen, just see, you cannot be disturbed; nothing exists which is separate from Buddha-mind or which can perturb you. Then, "even the waves break against it and are changed into light."

❧

> *Do not dwell on opposites.*
> *Do not seek out dualism.*

Master Dogen used to say, "When opposites arise, *bodaishin* is lost."

In the West, God and the ego are separate, whereas Zen is based on the harmony of the ego with everything that exists—with humanity, but, more profoundly, with Buddha. "Buddha" has a vast significance. It means not only Shakyamuni Buddha; not only the buddhas of the past, or the future buddha, Maitreya;

but also the mind of every great master right down to the present time. Practicing zazen is becoming Buddha. If you manage to let your thoughts pass, you notice this Buddhahood. You notice it when you stretch your spine, when you pull in your chin.

Bodaishin is Buddha-mind concentrated in the ego in the present moment. It's Buddha in each of us here and now.

So, no duality between Buddha and the ego. Without *bonnos*, the illusions of your ego, you cannot know awakening.

It's hard for people who doubt to accept the idea that we are One and that the ego is in unity with the cosmos; but deep down you have to have the certitude that you, I and the cosmos have one and the same root (in Zen, as you know, we're not interested in the leaves, but in the roots); and this certitude is faith in mind, which is not-two—*funi*.

If your mind separates you from Buddha (or God, if you prefer)—which is frequently the case—it is no longer the mind of faith that I'm talking about. And remember, it's not a matter of faith in something—in yourself, or in Buddha—but faith without object. This is exactly the attitude of *mushotoku*: no object, nothing to obtain. If the slightest notion of gain exists, the obstacle in your consciousness becomes very large.

❧

One translation of the kanji *zazen* is "two people on one zafu." Two opposites becoming a unity. The first time I heard Master Deshimaru explain this, I was very surprised; but today, it seems perfectly obvious: of course there are two people. "Two people" also means you're not practicing alone. You practice alone with others. You're completely alone, you're born alone and die alone, but the practice is to rediscover this solitude among others; and from there, we can be together intimately. Our practice is to be with others in silence, in *ku*, in nothing.

This zazen of not-two makes everything that is hesitant, vague or indecisive in your mind and your life disappear. Your concentration becomes strong and sharp, naturally and effortlessly.

And from this two that become One (and not even One—because Zen, starker than all other paths, ends up rejecting non-duality too), wisdom flows.

22

If you still have the slightest notion of right or wrong,
Your mind will sink into confusion.

This strophe isn't very complicated. It simply means that from the moment there is right or wrong, there is confusion. I would add that from the moment there is right or wrong, there is doubt—self-doubt. And because of these doubts, we adopt definitive positions: "I'm for, I'm against," "This is good, that's bad," "There's a man of satori! The other guy is really pathetic."

A wandering practitioner said to a master one day, "I only believe in ancient Ch'an."

"What do you mean by ancient Ch'an?" asked the master.

"I had satori on my own," replied the wandering practitioner, "not through zazen, not at all through the practice. I had it by myself, directly from the cosmos, with no intermediary. I've been going from place to place, looking for a Zen master who could confirm my satori, but unfortunately I haven't found one."

The master in question, an authentic master of the transmission, replied, "I myself have not had satori. So how can I certify you?"

The wanderer, who thought he knew everything, was very surprised, and filled with confusion.

～❀～

It's a mistake to choose too much. And anyway, bad can become good. One morning in the Paris Dojo, for example, there was no *genmai*, because the person in charge of it was on vacation. No problem: we were able to do zazen a little longer.

Don't choose. Choosing is an obstacle that blocks you from entering the Way. *Genmai*? No *genmai*? Doesn't matter.

The world of transmigration, *samsara*, is not only the world after death; it also functions in this very lifetime, precisely because of this choosing. That's why we're always coming back to the posture, to the exhalation, to observation: with zazen, our personal consciousness, the one that chooses, can tire itself out and leave room for cosmic consciousness. At that moment, cosmic awareness and the ego merge.

23

Two depends on One;
But do not be attached, even to One.

All dualities come from One; so drop that too. Don't even hang on to unity.

In Christianity and most other religions, there is One, the Absolute, God. But in Buddhism, we don't worry about this question: God, no God…. If you believe in God, that's fine. If you pray to God, that's fine. But while you're practicing zazen, don't get stuck on anything.

In zazen, we're in one thing, then another. That's normal. We're concentrating on zazen, but we don't stay with concentration—we also move on to observation. During zazen, the hypothalamus (instinctive brain) opens up, but we also have a frontal brain, and we go from one to the other. It's impossible to experience both phases simultaneously, any more than you could inhale and exhale at the same time. First one, then the other.

Staying with One, whatever that One is (and there are all kinds of Ones), means grabbing onto something, tying up your hands and feet. Almost everyone is hanging on to something: an idea, or God (the highest One); but it's the same as stagnating on a thought.

Your mind doesn't need a set of tracks. It's not a railroad. Swami Prabhavanda said, "If living by rule alone ensures excellence, if it be virtue strictly to follow the rules, say then, who is a greater devotee, a holier saint, than a railway train?"[13] No, the mind should be more like water, which flows freely and effortlessly. We don't practice to win or lose, to get to the next station or get away from the previous one, but to go deeper into the Way.

Master Fuyodokai said, "*Shukke* [literally, 'home-leavers'] should despise the dirty work of the mind [the small mind, obvi-

[13] Christopher Isherwood, *My Guru and His Disciple* (New York: Farrar, Straus, Giroux, 1980).

ously], be beyond life and death, stop the activity of the mind and reject all complicated relationships."

Because, in the final analysis, what's important in this practice—and in everyday life as well—is not to let your mind get stuck on anything. This way, you develop a light mind, free and detached. This doesn't mean indifferent; on the contrary, when you're not attached to One, compassion can appear.

"Even if a voice or a color seduces you, you must be like someone who plants flowers in stone," adds Fuyodokai. In other words, don't grow roots.

Zen Buddhism specialists think we want to become One—one with flowers, for example, one with everything that is One. But that's not exactly our practice; it's not Dogen Zen, and it's not the Zen we practice in the Deshimaru sangha. If we want to become One, it's a matter of personal will, and that's not the authentic teaching, that's not being led by the cosmic system. In fact, in Rinzai they even say, "When you see Buddha, kill him," which means, "Don't hold an illusory belief in a Buddha outside of yourself."

Don't be attached to Buddha or to yourself. Don't be attached to One either. This is absolutely Zen teaching: neither two—neither the right head nor the left head, neither good nor evil—nor One. In other words, not even the middle head, not even One, not even cosmic mind, not even God, not even Buddha.

∽◦

Two depends on One;
But do not be attached, even to One.

Here, *Two* means *shiki*, phenomena, substance; *One* means *ku*, emptiness. But *ku* is not oblivion. *Ku* is like the light that creates all colors, contains all colors, is all colors, but does not take on a single hue.

The passage I often cite from the *Hannya Shingyo*—*ku sokuze shiki, shiki sokuze ku*—is usually translated as "emptiness equals phenomena, phenomena equal emptiness." I have always found this idea of equality superficial. With this interpretation, you could easily fall into a kind of nihilism—thought bereft of meaning. Then one day, I had the good fortune to happen upon this line, taken from one of Master Deshimaru's kusen: "*Ku* is not equal to *shiki* and *shiki* is not equal to *ku*, but *ku* is in itself *shiki.*" This helped me understand that things—*shiki*—can be neutral, but are not necessarily nothing; their significance is *ku*.

So don't be attached to things: to the earth, rocks, rain, sun.... Don't be attached to existence or non-existence, don't hold onto the slightest notion of material and non-material, or Dharma and non-Dharma.

Of course, differences exist; and of course, similarities exist. But don't be attached to either difference or similarity, and don't even protect One.

24

If no mind appears,
Phenomena will be free from error.

Strophe 24 is the continuation of Strophe 23.

If no mind is created, or realized, or manifested by thinking, or even by non-thinking, then there is no error. We could also say that if no dualism and no monism are created, then there is no error. Or, if nothing is created, then there is no error.

Scholar R.H. Blyth translates the first line of this strophe as, "When the mind is one and nothing happens..."[14] "Nothing happens" is not an expression used in Zen practice, because it has a nihilistic connotation. But we can also understand it as the fundamental truth that "nothing increases, nothing decreases." This is undivided mind: there's nothing missing and nothing extra.

Sometimes putting things into different words makes them easier to understand. So I have tried to reformulate Strophe 24 in various ways:

If the mind is not set in motion,
Phenomena show no flaw.

When the mind functions on the Way, without disturbances,
nothing in this world can throw it into error.
And when nothing can throw it into error, phenomena cease
to exist,
or do not exist in the same way.

When the mind does not appear,
The ten thousand dharmas are flawless.

---

[14] *Zen and Zen Classics*, v. 1, p. 73.

Or even better,

The ten thousand dharmas are no longer troubled.

When the mind is unified, without being attached to anything,
The ten thousand things are harmless.

When you no longer have even the idea of mind,
Then there is nothing lacking or extra in this universe.

When your mind is no longer disturbed,
The ten thousand things no longer need to be rejected.

❧

This strophe is easy enough to understand. The mind that is set in motion is small mind: the one, for example, that lives only in the past or the future, or knows only success or failure. It's the mind that follows its thoughts. And when thoughts come up, the imagination starts working, and *bonnos* appear.

A samurai came to visit a Zen master to ask him a question that had been tormenting him for a long time. Naturally, this samurai didn't practice zazen. He devoted himself entirely to the way of the sword. His question seemed completely sincere.

"What is hell?" he asked the Zen master.

The Zen master told him he didn't feel like answering that question on that particular day.

"Why not?" asked the samurai.

"Because you're too stupid."

"What do you mean, too stupid?"

"You're too stupid. You wouldn't understand."

The samurai was offended. He was probably imagining what his lord, the shogun, would think if he saw him just then. So he tried to ask his question again, but the master cut him off.

"What could you possibly understand? You're a cardboard samurai! A loser!"

At that point, the samurai really got mad.

"And you! What are you? A good-for-nothing parish priest! A boot-licking Buddha-lover!"

"You're a coward!" laughed the Zen master.

"That's it," said the samurai. "I'm cutting off your head!"

He began to draw his sword. The master, completely unphased, laughed even harder.

"With what—a rubber sword?"

Trembling with rage, his face dripping sweat, the samurai raised his weapon over his head. Just as he was about to strike, the master pointed at him and said:

"There. That's hell."

When small mind appears and starts following thoughts and *bonnos*, it can sometimes go as far as murder. The mind is moving, following something, fixing on an idea and chasing it down. When that happens, illusions appear.

You can experience this during zazen. Look at yourself, look at your mind and follow your thoughts. Think, for example, of your favorite subject: sex, your husband, your wife, your children, a nice steak. Follow, say, the steak, for a little while. You'll quickly notice that your illusions increase. Then stop following the steak and follow your exhalation instead: long, deep and calm. The steak disappears, along with your mind.

The mind that disappears is the mind that ceases to appear. It's *mushin*, no-mind. This doesn't mean there's nothing there. Phenomena still exist. The earth is still here. But there are no more errors. Nothing missing, nothing extra. Just things as they are: *inmo*.

To avoid the continual appearance of small mind, we practice letting things pass, letting go. Zazen is the practice *par excellence* for letting go. When I teach during zazen, I always say, "Let your thoughts pass." When you practice zazen, all you have to do is sit in the correct posture, not lapse into sleep or agitation, and above all, not follow your thoughts. Just exhale slowly and deeply, without forcing.

But "let your thoughts pass" doesn't mean you shouldn't think or have a viewpoint. The mind that does not appear, that lets things go, is not a paralyzed, frozen mind, but a fluid mind that flows from change to change.

Letting your thoughts pass simply means practicing the Middle Way, which is not something lukewarm, situated between two extremes. The Middle Way is not *shiki* (phenomenon, form) or *ku* (emptiness, non-form). It's *shiki sokuze ku, ku sokuze shiki*: *shiki* becomes or is *ku*, and *ku* becomes or is *shiki*. This is not abstract; it is directly related to our existence as individuals. The Middle Way is surrendering yourself to every moment. Surrendering to what? Some people surrender to God or Buddha, but God or Buddha isn't what's important. In the end, they're just concepts, forms. Our practice isn't really interested in forms. What's important is the act of letting go, the act of *shin jin datsu raku*: throwing down body and mind.

One day, shortly after Master Deshimaru's death, one of my co-disciples wanted to do an advertisement for the Paris Dojo. He wanted to photograph someone in correct posture, preferably a young woman, and then use the picture as publicity. So he decided to contact a modeling agency. He studied the photos they offered, and said, "That one." To see if the young woman in question (a rather thin blonde) could get into the posture, he had her come to the dojo. She had never seen the zazen posture in her life. She was shown how to cross her legs, how to tilt her pelvis forward, how to hold her head and hands, how to pull in her chin. We were all dumbstruck: she did it absolutely perfectly—and on the first try! We took the photos.

Afterwards, we studied the pictures. The model seemed completely concentrated on her *tanden*, her shoulders were relaxed, her gaze was turned inward ... but something wasn't right. Maybe she didn't have enough *ki*; maybe she didn't have enough faith in what she was doing. We couldn't put our finger on it. But it was very interesting. Her posture was exemplary, the form was apparently perfect, and yet, beyond that, there was something missing, or something extra, a mistake, a fault, and it didn't work, even though we couldn't say exactly why.

Later on, we used the photos a little; they seemed to draw people who were not really interested in the practice, but more in the idea of the practice. However, people who were already practicing and knew the practice well were not happy with the photos. In the end, we completely stopped using them.

Drop everything—form and non-form—and practice the Middle Way. Neither *shiki* nor *ku*. That way you can observe all your problems and conflicts from a much higher point of view.

❧

In ancient times, the Middle Way was considered to be the Pleasure Way, meaning that it does not create suffering. This is not true Zen. Contrary to what you might read in books about Buddhism (especially ancient Buddhism), don't run away from suffering. Don't look for *samadhi* either. Don't practice zazen to improve your health or to find calm and tranquility. Just practice *shikantaza*: silent sitting, concentrating with no goal or object, *mushotoku*.

I think that if mistakes are made in zazen practice today, they are often connected to the notion of pleasure: the pleasure of the state of *mushin*, no-mind; the pleasure of the state of *samadhi*. Of course, pleasure is useful: it motivates us, it pushes us to participate in days of zazen and sesshin. It's obviously a pleasure that goes beyond the pleasure of eating or making love. But in the final analysis, it's still part of the same illusion.

You have to be careful not to let yourself be fooled by the pleasure of here and now; otherwise, you can bet it won't be long before mind appears and is set in motion, and you won't be on the Middle Way anymore. The Middle Way, Zen, is not the Way of Pleasure, even if it is pleasurable. "Zen," said Kodo Sawaki, "means losing yourself, losing everything." Thinking you can obtain something, or get any kind of benefit from Zen, is just superstition.

❧

The *Avatamsaka Sutra*, a Mahayana sutra, tells us that "everything is mind." This sutra tries to show us that Buddha, mind and sentient beings are the same thing; it teaches us that the whole universe is a single mind.

To put it another way, everything depends on your mind. If you eat too much: mind! If you never eat enough: mind! Is alcohol medicine or poison? Is money a treasure or a curse? It depends on your mind.

Only in the human mind can phenomena appear as errors or show faults. No error is possible if mind is not set in motion (as you can observe during zazen). As soon as mind is set in motion, everything changes, everything reacts. Even plants and flowers react to mind when it appears. They react to whatever isn't in the normal, original condition—not just the human condition, but the universal condition—because the whole universe is a single mind.

This is no abstraction or vague philosophical theory; this is an integral part of Mahayana teaching and directly concerns you. If the whole universe is a single mind, how, for example, do you see yourself in the midst of everyone else? How, in this world, do you see other people inside you?

Often people who practice criticize experienced practitioners and elder disciples, judging them from the outside. But if you really want to criticize somebody, the criticism should come from Buddha, from the buddha inside you, and not from your personal consciousness. A person who criticizes must be able to discern the other person's mind. It's not a question of his mind being good or bad—you'll never harmonize if you think in those terms—but a question of mind that appears or does not appear. If mind appears, it sees other people's faults, and other people's minds see your faults.

꙾

In the final analysis, *no mind appears* means that you're not being led by your personal awareness—which doesn't mean that you should do away with personal awareness and become a zombie.

Following your personal awareness leads to complications, which become more and more pronounced and can quickly cause mental problems. In fact, we're all familiar with this process, in ourselves or in others: this excessive awareness which, in the end, drives away the people around us.

Don't let yourself be guided by your personal awareness: that's the teaching of the twenty-fourth strophe. And the work that falls to each of us—master, monk or simple practitioner—consists of not feeding personal thoughts and not having an awareness that comes from the ego.

This doesn't necessarily mean that you shouldn't be guided by anything. The master-disciple relationship has existed since the most far-off times. The master represents what is universal in us: the undivided mind, with no inside or outside. Finally, this is what we can follow fearlessly, because this is the mind that does not appear and is not set in motion.

That's why I often say, "Don't be influenced by the environment; be influenced by the cosmic system instead." Be guided by the sky, by the earth, by the cosmic order, instead of by your personal awareness.

In his commentary on Strophe 24, Master Deshimaru says, "The cosmic system guides our lives, but these days, we think too much with our personal consciousness." So what should you do? How do you think not-thinking? How do you not-think thinking? Because if you think "I shouldn't think," that's the mind appearing and being set in motion.

"Unconsciously, naturally, automatically—that's Sensei's Zen!" Master Deshimaru once said, "I know I repeat it a lot, but it's very deep."

During zazen, unconsciously, naturally and automatically, thoughts come up, then disappear. This is the normal state, the normal condition, and it's not at all the same as following your personal consciousness.

Hotetsu was a Ch'an master from the Rinzai School, a disciple of Baso. One day, Hotetsu was sitting in front of the dojo, fanning himself with a fan. A monk appeared and questioned him. (At that time, monks asked each other a lot of questions, especially in Rinzai Zen.)

"Since wind blows everywhere, and its nature never changes, there is no reason to use a fan. Why do you do so?" asked the monk.

Some questions are very clever. The monk was saying that the nature of wind is everywhere, air is everywhere, and so he didn't understand the master's efforts to fan himself. He was undoubtedly referring to Buddha-nature, but he was stepping in a minefield.

"Though you know that the nature of wind never changes, you do not know what 'blows everywhere' means," replied Hotetsu.

Naturally, the monk was a little confused. He asked, "Okay, what does it mean?"

Hotetsu's answer was to continue fanning himself.

I think there are many ways to understand this little story. It could be related to *gyoji*, continuous practice, continuing what we do, with no goal. But, like many Zen stories, it is a metaphor for the Way, for cosmic energy. Cosmic energy—the wind—is everywhere; Hotetsu continued to fan himself and nothing was disturbed. Phenomena show no fault. That's what it means not to be mentally attached to structures. That's the mind that does not appear.

But if you don't welcome this wind, this cosmic energy, if you don't practice it with and through your own body, you cannot receive it. Only when you live in unity with the cosmic system can you be happy and free. Everywhere.

25

No error, no Dharma;
No Dharma, no mind.

That's the literal translation of the Japanese kanji.

This strophe of the *Shinjinmei* is very powerful. It shows us Zen as a steep cliff: it goes straight to the point. This is where the Dharma ceases to be necessary, where cosmic order and universal law become useless.

Here's what Master Yoka Daishi said about these two lines:

> *This opinion, this expression of non-fear,*
> *Explodes like the lion's roar.*
> *It bursts the brain*
> *Of the hundred animals who hear it.*

Here's a less abrupt translation of this strophe:

> *If there is no error, there is no Dharma;*
> *If there is no creation of Dharma, there is no mind.*

When error does not exist, the Dharma is not necessary, nor is order, or universal law: no God, no Jesus Christ, no Buddhist teaching.

Strophe 25 may seem harsh. From a Christian standpoint, it could even be interpreted as blasphemous: you say "no God," and immediately you're labeled an atheist. Yet it's another way of educating, teaching and giving, because "no God," like *No error, no Dharma*, simply means that there's no mind plunged into illusion, no stupid mind.

Most Western cultures have religions with holy days, like Sunday or the Sabbath. But other cultures are different. Native Americans, for example, have no particular holy day. There isn't even any religion as we know it, because they don't need any. No need for a holy day, no need for a church. It's the same in Zen. We don't need a Buddha statue: a big stone would be enough. We don't need a dojo: we can practice where we want. This doesn't mean that we don't need to be educated through a practice. Native Americans receive an education every day; they practice all the time. For them, all life is sacred; their whole lives are a practice. It's the same in Zen.

And so, far from being severe or nihilistic, this strophe is actually an expression of great compassion. It's not talking about nothing; it's talking about the essence. This essence has no noumenon. It is *ku*, empty, essence without noumenon.

No error, begins Strophe 25. No fault, no special essence. In other words, there is no God, no Buddha, that exists outside of us—which, in my opinion, goes deeper than the viewpoint adopted by Christianity.

"No special essence" means always coming back to yourself. Come back to the zazen posture, which follows the cosmic order, naturally, automatically and unconsciously. Come back to the position of your hands, the position of your eyes, the observation of your thoughts.

In the end, there is no Buddha, no master. As the anarchists say, "Neither God nor master." No mind—*mushin*.

Master Dogen explains that *mushin* is the source of all minds, of all forms of mind. He also says that the true Buddhist mind, in other words, an undivided mind, lies beyond discriminations and oppositions.

This is the inner revolution, the 180-degree turn which frees you from yourself, and which is perhaps neither positive nor negative. Is freedom from yourself—from your ego, your small ego—a positive thing? Maybe being happy through your breathing is not positive, because the idea of positive and negative is always a concept that springs from the small mind.

The fundamental root of Buddhism is *kakunen musho*. *Kakunen* means "infinite, open sky"; *musho*, "no holiness, no madness." There is no more holiness in silence—which we sometimes call golden—than there is in the sound of a hammer. With silence, you can hear your breathing; with the noise from a hammer, you can hear the hammer talking to the nail.

It is said in the *Diamond Sutra*, "When the mind dwells on nothing, true mind appears." This is the teaching, this is what we should practice—with our breathing, with our postures, with our bodies. It's the state of *hishiryo*—beyond thinking, beyond mind.

Hishiryo is a concept which is very present in Buddhism, especially Zen. In his comments on Strophe 25, Master Deshimaru described this state this way: "You should be like a dead person in a coffin. When everything disappears, consciousness vanishes."

This means dropping your *bonno*, your illusions. Drop everything: Buddhism, Zen, even zazen. Forget the self, forget the mind.

Here's a poem from Master Dogen's *Eiheikoroku*:

> *Go beyond the buddhas and the patriarchs of all time.*
> *Do not be attached to south or north or east or west.*
> *Eat the rice cake with the intuition of the wind and clouds.*
> *Attack and strike the sage.*

Master Dogen's "strike the sage" was perhaps inspired by Master Rinzai, who said, "Kill the Buddha." He may also have been thinking of the monk, Fuke, who ran through the streets clanging his little bell and singing,

> *Strike the light when it approaches shade.*
> *When it comes from the south, the north, the east,*
> *the west, the eight directions,*
> *I attack like a whirlwind.*
> *I strike it with my broom.*
> *Ding! Ding! Ding!*

Eno was born in Canton, in southern China. One day, he heard a monk reciting the *Diamond Sutra*: "When the mind dwells on nothing, true mind appears." He was inspired to seek the Way, and, on the monk's suggestion, went to see Zen master Konin, who lived in the Eastern Mountain Temple.

He arrived at the temple and Master Konin asked him, "Where do you come from?"

"From the south," answered Eno.

"The south?" said Konin. "Oh my poor boy, I'm afraid you don't understand a thing!"

"It's true, I come from the south," replied Eno, "but on the Way there is no north or south."

All this to say that, in the end, there is no measure, no Buddha, no Dharma. It doesn't matter if you come from the south or north, east or west, because the real question Konin asked Eno is, "How far are you from your original nature?"

❧

In Buddhism, south, north, east and west don't mean anything. They're categories, relative expressions. Buddha, Dharma, and even sangha are just nice words. For a lot of people, they're comforting, but in reality they're empty of noumenon. They're just fingers pointing to the moon.

Here's what Master Dogen says in his *Zazenshin*: "The essence of Zen is transmitted from buddha to buddha and master to master. It is fulfilled without conceptualization and accomplished without causality."

When a disciple—monk, bodhisattva, layperson—practices seriously, every day, then words like "buddha," "dharma" and "*ku*" are just concepts. Whereas for someone who does not practice, but teaches nevertheless, "Buddhism" and "Buddha" are reality. That's why the more you practice Buddhism, the harder it is to talk about.

And so we have the expression *tokusho*, which means "a place beyond verbal expression." This has nothing to do with the scholar, professor or writer, who earns his living by putting everything into words. For them, words become reality. For people who practice, Buddha turns the flower in his hand and Mahakashyapa smiles.

❧

No error, no Dharma.
No Dharma, no mind.

122

No *ku*, no *shiki*... What is it? Here's a poem by Ryokan:

> *Wherever I am, I am home.*
> *It is no different than Bodhidharma's Mount Sung.*
> *Riding out the changes that each new day brings,*
> *I spend the years of my life in calmness and freedom.*

This is simply the normal condition, the original condition, what is. "Riding out the changes"—*mujo*.

People who deeply understand *mujo* are never unhappy. Because for such people, every thought is a good thought. The content of the thought is not good or bad, but every thought in itself is a good thought. Why? Because the man of the Way, the woman of *mujo*, simply sees the thought appear, then disappear. That way, wherever they are, they are home, riding out the changes.

This is *doshu*—the expression of true freedom.

26

Following the object, the subject vanishes;
Following the subject, the object collapses.

Although the *Shinjinmei* is more poetic than many other ancient Zen texts, certain strophes, in my opinion, aren't very poetic at all. When Master Deshimaru translated them, he wasn't worried about poetry. This is especially true for Strophes 26 through 29, which deal with *subject* and *object*—typical Zen terminology. If you want to understand Buddhism, if you want to be able to teach it, you must really grasp this question of subject and object.

It has been said that this strophe is a koan; but I don't see why, since it can be more or less explained, whereas a koan is inexplicable. For example, how do you explain the sound of one hand clapping?

✼

When the subject disappears, the object disappears as well; when the object disappears, the subject disappears too. Or: when the thought disappears, the thought object disappears as well, and vice versa.

Master Dogen taught that all our thoughts are illusory. They rely on objects or symbols. And when you don't have those mental objects inside your mind anymore, your *bonnos*—illusory forms—disappear. *Bonno soku bodai*: illusion becomes satori.

Ryutan had been with his master, Tenno Dogo, for three years. One day, he told him:

"Up until now, Master, you have taught me nothing."

"What?" replied the master. "In all the times you've come here, when did I not teach you something?"

"Oh really? You taught me something?"

"Every time you served me tea, every time you brought me something to eat, I bowed my head."

Ryutan began to think about this. So the master added:
"When you look, just look. If you try to understand, you'll never make it."

The disciple who tries to understand is a subject that appears, a mind that manifests. As soon as there are no more mental objects in his mind, then this subject, this ego, disappears. There are no more illusory thoughts, no more "faults."

In a way, Strophe 26 echoes Strophe 24, which says, "No mind, no error." Here, it's "When things don't exist anymore, neither does mind; when mind doesn't manifest, things don't manifest either."

One night Master Nansen decided to visit two farmers living near his hermitage. He made his decision all alone at home, and mentioned it to no one; but the next day, when he arrived at the farm, to his great astonishment he found the farmers—and an enormous feast—waiting for him.

"Who is this meal for?" he asked with surprise.

"It's for you, Master!" replied one of the farmers.

"But how did you know I was coming?"

"Late last night, an earth god announced your arrival today. So we prepared this meal."

"I am ashamed," replied Nansen. "My practice must be very poor if the gods are able to spy on what happens in my head!"

In Buddhist legend, there are several kinds of gods who have no trouble entering the heads of people (even monks) who are not sufficiently attentive to the functioning of their minds. Ashamed that these gods were able to see his mind when it moved, Nansen returned to his hermitage, where he meditated on this question for a long time. Maybe he re-read Strophe 24 or 26 of the *Shinjinmei*, which had been composed one hundred and fifty years before he was born and was known by all the masters of that period. Whatever the case may be, he began to practice seriously alongside his disciples. He practiced letting his thoughts pass—*mushin*, no-mind—so well that they died before the gods could see them.

And then one day, the gods came to see Nansen. But they couldn't find the master, although he was sitting peacefully at home in zazen. Nansen had become invisible to them. And why was he invisible? Simply because his mind was not moving. It did not manifest anymore in any way. He was not at all influenced by the environment, or attached to any kind of mental object.

I imagine that a wise person would be inclined to think about this question of moving mind at the moment of his or her death. Because if you have a lot of mental objects when you're about to die, it will be difficult for you to control the direction your mind will go in after death.

Your karma always leads you in the direction of your strongest desires and attachments. Generally, this is the baggage, the accumulation of mental objects, that you carry around in your head for your whole life—often, unfortunately, right up to the moment of death. (This is especially the case for people who commit suicide.) This personal karma will control your impetus and direction, even after death.

So how can you be free when you're about to die? How can you be free in this lifetime? How can you be free here and now? How can you not be bound hand-and-foot by mental objects, desires and attachments?

⚓

When the gods went into his house, Nansen was practicing zazen exactly: *shikantaza*, precise, silent sitting. Just that, without goal, without anything. *Mu.*

And so, when you understand Strophe 26, you can also understand the exact attitude of mind during zazen. The subject (the self) that vanishes when following the object (the outside), and vice versa, is the fluid mind which, during zazen, does not dwell on anything, going endlessly from non-form (*ku*) to form (*shiki*) and back again.

This strophe is the mind during zazen. When "one" disappears, "other" does too. The subject disappears with the object; the object disappears with the subject. Imagine, for example, that you're sitting in zazen, and you hear music. If you go with the music—not running away from it, not running after it—then the music disappears. There is no separation between subject and object, no dualistic relationship. During zazen, there's no point in thinking about God or not-God. It's better to look into yourself.

Don't go anywhere but into yourself. That's where God is. That's where Buddha is.

There's no point in making a separation between zazen and daily life, either, or between inside and outside the temple, or between the dojo and the street. Though the street may avoid the dojo, the dojo—the practice—does not avoid the street. It doesn't run off to the Himalayas. The practice changes the mind. As it happens, the world—the whole universe—is contained in the mind. The mind changes, the world changes. And when the mind vanishes, the object, the world, vanishes as well. There's no separation between mind and world.

This is what you can experience during zazen. After one, two or ten years of practice, what happens? *Mushin*, no mind. Individual karma is cut. It's Nansen becoming invisible. It's true freedom.

༄

Following the object, the subject vanishes;
Following the subject, the object collapses.

Subject and object fall together.
Here are a few paraphrases I formulated of Strophe 26:

When things cease to exist, mind does the same.
When mind disappears, things do the same.

When thought objects disappear, you disappear.
And when your mind disappears, its objects disappear.

No more subject, no more object;
No more object, no more subject.

The observer disappears after the observed.
And vice versa.

When your skull, filled to bursting, empties itself,

*Your mind is simply a vehicle from which thoughts appear
and disappear.*

*No more cosmos, no more spectator;
No more spectator, no more cosmos.*

Subject means "ego," "personal consciousness"; *object* means
"environment," "cosmic consciousness," "other existences." So
Strophe 26 is telling us about the harmony between the ego and
the cosmos.

In his commentary, Master Deshimaru says, "When our ego
has noumenon, the environment—in other words, the cosmic
system—appears." "Noumenon" is a synonym for "substance."
"When your ego has substance"—but this is obviously an illusion,
since the ego has no substance. Let"s say, "If you think your ego
has substance and you function with this idea, then the cosmic
system appears."

When I read this quotation from Master Deshimaru for the
first time, I was disturbed and perplexed. "When our ego has
noumenon, the cosmic system appears." What could it possibly
mean? First I thought it was a typing mistake, or a mistake in the
note-taking. But still, I wasn't sure. So I spent an hour repeating
the sentence to myself. Since I still didn't understand, I put my
head under cold water. But that didn't work. Then I put on my
rakusu. Still no result. So I had a glass of whiskey. And then, suddenly, I understood.

Seeing the cosmic system appear is the subject manifesting;
by so doing, it creates the object. Sosan, in Strophe 26, tells us that
the cosmic system must not appear; the subject should vanish, following the object, and vice versa. If the subject does not vanish, if
it keeps the substance of its ego—in other words, when the ego is
really the ego—then the object, the cosmic system, appears. And
not only the cosmic system, but everything—God, Buddha, me.

On the other hand, if you don't look at the world through
your ego, then nothing appears; there is no cosmic system. Why?
Because there is no more subject, and therefore, no more object.

Kodo Sawaki once defined satori as a thief going into an empty house: there's nothing left to steal.

✧

Men and women of satori, of awakening, of the Way, never see the cosmic system appear, because they don't function with the idea that the ego has noumenon. They don't look at the world with their egos. They don't talk about the cosmic system, or about satori; they don't say, "The cosmic system is like this or like that." In fact, they don't even know they have satori; a buddha doesn't know he's Buddha. This reminds me of a saying attributed to Dogen's master, Eisai: "Only cattle and cats know they are Buddha."

Someone I knew once overheard Zen disciples talking together in a café. They were just talking about ordinary things, she told me, not at all about life, morality, good or evil. She seemed very disappointed. I suppose she would have preferred to hear a discussion about philosophy or religion. But they just went on talking about what was happening in the here and now.

Master Deshimaru said that satori comes "from the outside," in the sense that, for example, when Buddha Shakyamuni had his great satori, the entire universe had satori; there was no more separation between him and the cosmos, between subject and object.

That's *funi*, not-two. It's the unity between satori and the functioning of the cosmos. Shakyamuni saw the morning star and, in that instant, he experienced supreme satori, the supreme vehicle. And this supreme vehicle is not the vehicle of the bodhisattva. It's not the vehicle of the *shomon* either, or that of the *engaku*. This vehicle that we try to practice is not the vehicle of celestial beings, either, the *devas*. And it is obviously not the vehicle of men and women. This vehicle is not something we can grasp through thought or non-thought.

This supreme vehicle, this satori, as grandiose as it may sound, is nothing other than our true original nature, which existed before our life on earth and will exist after it. It is nothing other than the mind during zazen, beyond the personal, beyond the person, beyond subject and object, automatically, unconsciously and naturally.

That's why all the masters of the transmission say that zazen is satori. Master Dogen, for example, was always repeating that zazen and satori are not different, that satori does not come afterwards, nor does zazen come before. And Master Deshimaru's commentary continues this way: "The forgetting of the self through personal will is very difficult to accomplish. But by concentrating on the posture and breathing, we can abandon our personal consciousness." That means that you cannot forget your self, your ego, through self-will. Harmony between the self and the cosmos can only be realized unconsciously and naturally, outside of conscious will. *Following the object, the subject vanishes*, and the small ego becomes the big ego, the cosmic ego.

Unlike many other masters, Master Deshimaru didn't talk about reincarnation. Here's what he said one day in the dojo about death and rebirth: "When we die, when our breathing stops, if our last thought follows the cosmic system, our consciousness is in union with it and our imagination can reach the depths of the cosmos."

27

The object can be fulfilled as a true object
through its dependence on the subject.
The subject can be fulfilled as a true subject
through its dependence on the object.

The next three strophes are closely linked to Strophe 26, and also talk about subject and object. They are completely interdependent.

If you know how to decode them, the *Shinjinmei* strophes are not as complicated as they may seem. In general, they describe the awakened mind. Here, it's the mind that makes no discriminations and yet sees all differences in a perfectly clear way.

Strophe 26 said that when the mind (the subject) disappears, the object disappears too, and vice versa. In Strophe 27, Sosan goes one step further and tells us the object is the cause of the subject, and vice versa.

The word *subject*, as we've seen, is used in the sense of "ego," "self" or "personal consciousness." It's the subject that has the possibility to see, hear, smell, taste, touch and think. *Object* can be understood as "environment," "other existences," or "the cosmic system."

So, the object appears as it does because of the subject.

Master Deshimaru said, "When we are alone, the need for an object disappears. If we are not looking, the object does not become concrete." In other words, there is only a true object if a subject appears.

To put it another way, by manifesting ourselves, we create things; and things, by manifesting themselves, create us. Subject and object—for example, myself and others—have therefore only a relative existence.

One day, Akbar, a Mogol emperor, drew a line on a wall. After this, he called the wisest men of his entourage and said to them, "Without touching this line, make it smaller." The men did not understand, they thought it was impossible. But suddenly Birbal, the wisest of wise men, drew a second line next to the first, which was slightly bigger. And so without being touched, the original line became smaller.

That's relative existence.

Subject and object are always relative. For example, hearing, or rather listening, creates sound: mind, the subject, creates noise and noise creates mind. Thus, if rain is rain, it's because of mind; if mind is mind, it's because of rain. One depends on the other.

But for someone sitting in zazen, abandoning themselves completely to the exhalation, noise does not create the person practicing, any more than the person practicing creates noise. For that person, rain and noise disappear. Everything disappears. This is *mushin*, no-mind. So what's left? Zazen? No, not even zazen.

Here's how Master Ejo described zazen: "If you abandon yourself to the exhalation and let your inhalation fill you up in a harmonious coming-and-going, there remains only a zafu under the empty sky. The weight of a flame."

Maybe death is nothing more than that.

∽❀∾

Let's get back to Sosan, who tells us that mind is mind because of things, because of objects. I think we've all experienced this at one time or another. In Zen, we call this certification: when the subject, the disciple's mind, is certified by the object.

I've never heard of anyone who was certified by the object without having practiced the Way of zazen under the guidance of an authentic master. Mahakashyapa's mind was certified by Buddha turning a flower in his hand. Master Deshimaru's mind was certified by his master Kodo Sawaki. And this certification of the disciple by the master takes place outside of any structure, religious or otherwise.

We could say that satori is "he who is certified plus he who certifies"—in other words, the person who experiences (the subject) plus the experience itself. Therefore, it's never the subject by itself, but subject and object, subject and cosmic system, subject and all phenomena.

I've never heard of a Zen story, for example, in which a master or a disciple sitting in zazen had inner satori, certified by him alone on his zafu.

What happens in zazen is that by looking into yourself, you forget yourself. And it's only then that you can awaken to the ten thousand dharmas. Follow your exhalation, practice *mushotoku*, no object, no goal, let your thoughts pass…and then the cosmic system (the object) can penetrate your personal consciousness (the subject)—unconsciously, naturally and automatically.

Buddha, when he had his satori, was practicing zazen under the *bodhi* tree. He was practicing *shikantaza* exactly, following his breath. And that's when he saw the morning star. It was certification by the object, by the cosmic system. It was the transmission, the *shiho*. It was the object that came to meet the subject, or, we could say, which entered into the subject. This has nothing to do with psychology, or even Buddhism. It's simply transmitted experience.

One day, a monk said to Master Joshu, "The moon is shining in the sky." (At that time, a lot of talking was done in symbols or metaphors. The shining moon is satori, or Buddha-nature.)

"You are under the roof (in other words, you are on Earth)," replied Joshu, "and the moon is in the sky."

"How, then, can I come into contact with the moon?" asked the disciple.

"The moon will come to meet you," said the master.

And so, looking into yourself does not bring about realization; satori doesn't come from the inside, but from the outside, the exterior. And those who think that satori comes from the inside have only personal satori.

In Zen, you often hear expressions like, "certified by the object," "certified by the cosmos," "certified by nature." And there are many Zen stories on this subject, monks who have satori by observing something, or hearing an external noise: they look at a star or hear the sound of the river in the valley, and they have an awakening.

At the simple sight of a peach blossom, Master Reiun achieved satori.

Sotoba had satori contemplating the mountains and hearing the sound of the valley. He wrote this poem immediately afterwards:

> *The sound of the valley is a great lecture.*
> *The color of the mountain is the true Buddha.*

Kyogen was a disciple of Isan, and a sutra specialist. One day, Isan said to him, "Talk to me about the self. Please, Kyogen, explain to me what self existed before the birth of your parents." Not knowing how to respond, Kyogen went back to his sutras; but he could not find the answer there. In despair, he took all his books and threw them into the fire. Someone asked him, "Whatever are you doing?" "A painting of a rice cake cannot satisfy hunger!" he replied. "From now on, I will spend my time working in the kitchen and making rice cakes." And that's what he did for years.

One day, he told his master Isan, "I am completely stupid! Please Master, tell me a word that will show me the path and open my mind." Isan replied, "Sure, I could tell you something. But if I do, later on you'll reproach me for it." Kyogen left Isan's dojo. He went into the mountains where he built a hermitage and grew bamboo.

Later, when he was sweeping the floor, a pebble knocked up against a stalk of bamboo—clack! It was exactly the right moment: when a chick is ready to be born, its mother breaks the shell. Kyogen did *sampai* in the direction of his master (Isan's dojo was situated at the foot of the mountain, on the other side of the valley) and said, "If you had given me an answer to my stupid question, I would never have had satori."

Then he wrote this poem:

> *My actions leave no trace.*
> *This is the true Way.*

Strophe 27 is therefore the realization of the body through all phenomena. The morning star, the peach blossom, the voice of the valley, the sound of the pebble against bamboo... and for the man or woman of satori, for the awakened mind, there is no more separation, no more subject-object duality.

In Zen, we attach a lot of importance to phenomena. The approach to life is not the same as in Christianity, where we are told what we have to do, how to do good, how to help. In Buddhism, it's more a matter of profoundly and intuitively understanding the nature of phenomena—how things work—and thus do what is necessary naturally and unconsciously.

This brings us right to Strophe 28.

28

If you wish to understand subject and object,
In the end you must realize that both are ku.

This means that if you want to grasp the two aspects that strophes 26 and 27 talk about—subject and object—you must understand that their origin is always one: one single and same *ku*. Object and subject are separate in duality: "You are under the roof and the moon is in the sky," said Joshu. Naturally, this duality is necessary: without it, we wouldn't be able to talk; without such words as "good" and "bad," we would be incapable of expressing ourselves; without the opposition between good and evil, for example, we wouldn't be able to write books.

We are also very different from each other, and Western culture (novels, films, etc.) speaks of nothing but this difference. Since we're not really interested in similarity, we forget about it.

The purpose of Strophe 28 is therefore to bring the two aspects of duality back to one unique and identical *ku*, without denying them; because as Sosan tells us, in the final analysis, difference is reduced to sameness.

For example, men and women are different. In the martial arts, a man is never made to fight a woman. It's the same in sports: women are ranked in a separate category. Nevertheless, says Sosan, both are originally identical and similar. And this is the mind of *ku*, the mind we experience during zazen: "One, unique *ku*, only zazen," said Master Deshimaru.

In zazen, we practice the essence, the root: where body and mind, man and woman, are identical; where differences are erased or fade away. During a sesshin, for example, we go from *shiki* to *ku*: *shiki sokuze ku*. *Shiki* becomes *ku*. Zazen after zazen, we return little by little to the normal condition; bit by bit, the problems we were carrying around in our minds at the beginning of the sesshin lose their importance; our thoughts decrease; the subject/object duality becomes much less pronounced. And when we return to our daily life, even if differences reappear—*ku* becomes *shiki*—there's no reason to fall into confusion.

So in the dojo, who's stronger on the zafu: men or women? There's no difference, no duality. The original is One.

But saying that difference ends up being reduced to sameness does not mean that everything is the same, or that we are all alike. It's easy to say, "We're all brothers and sisters." But it's not true. How can we be brothers and sisters when some of us are called "Serb" or "Croat" or "Israeli" or "Palestinian" or "American" or "Iraqi" or "Muslim" or "Buddhist" or "Christian"? Here, the definitions themselves carry hate. The Muslims say, "We are Muslim," the Hindus say, "We are Hindu," and what happens? The Muslims attack the Hindus, who in turn attack the Buddhists. They both practice self-identification, which is the opposite of what we teach: in Zen, we practice a kind of non-identification, which simply means living without limitations.

So in the end, what is difference? What is duality? What differentiates men from women, or a buddha from a demon?

True spiritual practice goes beyond differences. Man, woman, buddha, demon: it's the same thing. That's the true Zen teaching as Taisen Deshimaru, Kodo Sawaki and all the patriarchs transmitted it to us.

Here is a poem by Master Ikkyu that illustrates Strophe 28 very well:

> *Rain, hail, snow and ice*
> *Are different from each other,*
> *But once they fall,*
> *They form the same river in the valley.*

Self, others, subject, object: one unique and identical *ku*. So don't create separations between subject and object, between yourself and others.

✥

Ungo Doyo had been following a Buddhist master for several years. At his side, he studied the sutras and the patriarchs' writings. One day he said, "I'm sick of all this! Why would a normal man remain bound up by all these rules and laws?" (Many monks who later became masters—Dogen, for example—asked themselves the same question.)

Ungo left to live alone in the mountains. He did zazen in a hermitage and lived in complete ecstasy. His practice became so pure that nature took care of him: celestial beings came to bring him food. He didn't eat meat, didn't smoke, didn't make love. Only zazen.

One day, a monk passing through spoke to him of Master Tozan, one of the most famous Soto masters of the time. Ungo decided to go visit him in his dojo—just like that, no reason (he wasn't a Zen monk yet, but he was already practicing *mushotoku*).

Upon seeing him, Master Tozan asked, "What is your name?"

Ungo replied, "My name is Ungo."

"Beyond this name, who are you?"

Ungo, who was not stupid, replied, "Beyond, even Ungo cannot be named."

Tozan smiled and said, "It's the same response that I gave my master Ungan. If you like, you can stay here."

Ungo stayed for a while. One day, he asked Tozan, "What is the significance of the patriarchs' teaching?"

Tozan replied, "Later, when you are back in your hermitage, if someone asks you this question, what will you answer?"

Only someone who does not practice can explain Buddha-nature; for the practitioner, there is no way to do it. Ungo, understanding his error, had satori. He went back home to the mountains and began doing zazen again, but differently. The nature of his zazen completely changed. And from that moment on, the celestial beings who used to bring him things to eat stopped coming.

What happened? Before his encounter with Master Tozan, Ungo Doyo was in subject/object duality. He was nature's object; nature took care of him. Now, he *was* nature … and he had become invisible because of it.

Subject/object: one unique and identical *ku*. This is the state of non-separation, non-identification. It is also the source of real love.

❧

138

So stay away from all nationalism and categories. Don't be separate from other existences, from things, from the cosmos. Don't be special—on the contrary, as the Taoist master Chuang Tzu said, "Be ordinary."

In Zen, satori isn't interesting at all, even though a lot of people attach enormous importance to it, talk a lot about it and even write books on the subject. Kodo Sawaki warns us that "having a satori or two is no better than a fart." What's important is what happens afterwards. After Buddha had satori, he went off in search of companions—companions in satori, in other words, people he could share with. "Without companions in satori," he said, "it is very difficult to go on living."

But satori itself does not distinguish you from others in any way; on the contrary, you lose your friends, the tigers and birds forget you, you become invisible. All of a sudden, you're not special at all; you're just ordinary. You've just found the normal condition—one unique and identical *ku*.

I've already told the story of Master Gozu, who received flowers from the birds and was protected by tigers. One day, he met Master Doshin, and, like Ungo Doyo with Master Tozan, had satori after a mondo. What happened then? Exactly the same thing as with Ungo: the birds stopped bringing him flowers and the tigers kept away from him. This story happened in the 600s. Some two centuries later, a monk asked Master Joshu, "Why did the birds stop bringing flowers to Master Gozu after he met Master Doshin?"

Master Joshu replied, "One gets tired looking for firewood and carrying water."

This is a deep exchange. Being ordinary: in the end, maybe that's true Zen. And ordinary doesn't mean common, banal or unoriginal, but simply realizing that "the two are originally one," that "the two are one unique and identical *ku*."

This is how, in Buddhism, we go beyond the borders and boundaries of subject/object, and beyond the boundaries of the individual. We even go beyond the center. The origin and original nature of all things being *ku*, there is neither dualism nor monism. No left, no right and no middle either.

And so the idea is deeply to understand contradictions and differences; not to worry about them, not to deny them—because they do exist—but simply go beyond them.

⁂

Here is Ryokan's death poem:

The maple leaf falls
Showing now one side
Now the other.

Sometimes you have to make a decision. But that doesn't mean choosing one side or the other. It's not easy, because our minds are always in duality. Contradiction reigns between the frontal brain and the instinctive brain, and between left brain and right brain. But the broader your mind is, the easier it is to accept contradictions and transcend them. Then it's no longer a question of rationality, but a question of faith. This is zazen practice: going with faith beyond dualism and differences.

Which brings us to Strophe 29.

29

A ku identical to both
Includes all phenomena.

To put it another way, in *ku*, two (object and subject) are the same (*funi*) and contain all phenomena.

Master Deshimaru's commentary on this strophe is very succinct. He says that this is a very big Soto Zen koan, the source of Zen: *shikantaza*.

This strophe develops and deepens Strophe 28. It describes the mind—*ku*—that does not discriminate but nevertheless sees all phenomena clearly. It is not easy to apprehend, but if you really understand what *ku* is, it becomes less complicated. And obviously, you have to study these kinds of words unconsciously—not with your frontal brain.

༄

So what is *ku*?

Literally, the Japanese word *ku* means "sky." It is often translated as "emptiness," "vacuity" or "nothingness"; but I find all of these inadequate, so I continue to use the term *ku*, as Master Deshimaru did. Because *ku*, like the sky, is not empty. The sky contains mountains, oceans, rivers, streams, you and me. In other words, it contains two (subject and object); it contains everything.

Ku is essence without noumenon, without substance. One of the Buddha's most profound observations, still surprising today, is: "There is no *atman*." *Atman* is Sanskrit for "the immortal self," something like the soul, something absolute, an absolute consciousness, God. Saying that there is nothing absolute, nothing with substance, does not mean that, in the world of *ku*, the existence of things is denied. It's very important to really understand this, because if you think that things don't exist, you can easily fall into nihilism, which says that nothing is real, everything is empty. In fact, Zen has often been accused of being a nihilistic philosophy, especially in the West when the Christians began to discover Buddhism. But that's a very inaccurate view.

So what is real *ku*? Real *ku* is not *ku*. Impossible. Real *ku* is obviously *shiki*. This isn't a paradox, or a contradiction, or an attempt to be enigmatic; it's pure lucidity. It's what Sosan is saying in this strophe: *ku* is not only One. Because in *ku*, two (subject and object) are inseparable and indistinguishable; both include all phenomena.

Strophe 29 therefore shows us the interdependence of all things; each thing, each person, is the entire world. Our minds must include everything, because the truth is not found in one thing or another.

A wave, for example, is not separate from the ocean. It contains the ocean within itself. Obviously, the wave's form differs from the ocean's—there is separation—but in terms of existence, there is no distinction. The wave and the ocean are the same thing. The wave is the ocean and the ocean is the wave. You can't distinguish between them; one can't exist without the other.

Thus, *shiki* is in itself *ku* and *ku* is in itself *shiki*. And it's not an abstraction, either; this concerns our everyday lives, which I think would be much easier if we could profoundly understand this teaching.

Together, *shiki* and *ku* form the cosmos, and you should embrace both of them. No need to choose one side rather than the other. Don't be attached to *shiki*, going from thought to thought, phenomenon to phenomenon; and don't stagnate in *ku*, going from non-phenomenon to non-phenomenon.

We know all the stories of people who get attached to phenomena—you just have to look around, or better yet, look inside yourself. Today, we know the *shiki* side very well: we want to succeed, we want to get things. And when it comes to getting things, we can be very clever. Even wanting to progress in zazen is wanting to get something; it's separating *shiki* from *ku*. "I'm not progressing. I've been practicing for ten years and I'm still just as selfish."

We always want to clutter our lives with things, including things like emptiness and non-emptiness. The truth is, people who are attached to *ku*, who separate themselves from the world or try to escape it, are not so different from those who hang on to their thoughts, to phenomena, to things. Because when you become attached to something, you deny the other side—and you lose everything.

A Ch'an monk had been practicing *tso-chan* (Chinese for "zazen") for twenty years, in a small hut belonging to an old woman who fed him and saw to his needs. He practiced a lot of zazen. When he'd had enough of zazen, he chanted the *Hannya Shingyo*; when his knees hurt, he did *kinhin*. This had been going on for twenty years.

The old woman wondered a lot about him: she wondered where he was really at in terms of the practice, the normal condition, sex, desire, etc. One day she had an idea. She contacted a young woman who was "rich in desires."

"Go see the monk in the hut," said the old woman. "Go kiss him. And then, once you've kissed him, ask him, 'Now what?'"

The young woman—beautiful, seductive, sensual—brought the monk something to eat, caressed him, kissed him, then asked him, "Now what? What's up?"

Apparently, nothing was up.

She returned to see the old woman, who asked, "So, how did he react?"

"He said, 'An old dry tree, a cold rock in winter.'" (A poetic way of saying, "Go ahead and kiss me, I don't care. I don't feel anything for you.")

The old woman was very displeased.

"What a stupid monk! How could I have wasted years protecting him, that cold rock?!"

And that very same day, she chased him out and burned down the hut.

But then, how should the monk have reacted? This story does not mean that he should have made love to the young woman. Erection or no erection, what the monk was missing was understanding and compassion. No compassion, no love; no love, no real wisdom. He was too attached to his own idea of his practice of *ku*. He denied existence and created discrimination—young woman/true monk, sex/abstinence. In a word, he wasn't practicing anything worthwhile. That's the message of this old story.

This monk's behavior goes completely against the teaching of Strophe 29:

A ku identical to both
Includes all phenomena.

And so, there's no need to distinguish between *shiki* and *ku*; light contains all colors but is itself colorless. No need to distinguish between the sound of words, noise, the wind in the pine trees. No need to distinguish between immaterial and material, because material is immaterial in its essence. When you look at something very closely, you see molecules; but if you look even closer, you see nothing: *ku*. No need to distinguish between life and death, because there's no difference between them. By deeply understanding this, you can be happy in life and in death.

In the *"Genjokoan"* chapter of the *Shobogenzo*, Master Dogen talks about the relationship between life and death. He uses the example of wood and ashes. Wood, the tree in the forest, becomes ashes; and when the wood has become ash, it cannot go back to the state of wood: it's over. Life becomes death. "Ashes do not return to wood," says Dogen. In the same way, your death as an individual never becomes your own life again.

Yet Buddhism does not say that wood comes first and ashes follow, nor that birth comes before and death afterwards. You're not a person before and a pile of dust after. This way of seeing just comes from personal ideas. Because, though the wood and the person carry within them a before and an after, they belong to a dharmic dimension which is situated beyond before and after. "We must understand that wood remains in its dharmic position of wood," says Dogen.

The apparent contradiction here—and Dogen puts his finger squarely on it in the *"Genjokoan"*—is that on one hand, there is continual change, *mujo*, the impermanence of all things; and on the other hand, there is non-birth, non-death, eternity, *ku*, essence without noumenon. This is not contradictory, because both sides are correct. It's not life on one side and death on the other; *ku* is not one thing and *shiki* another.

Here's a poem by Eno, the sixth patriarch:

Sitting or lying, this whole pile of stinking bones—
In the end, what does it mean to you?
The body comes and goes,
Original nature always stays the same.

Of course, as individuals, we die—we return to *ku*, to the cosmic order. And we don't come back from this *ku*—no more *shiki*. But from a wider perspective, Buddhism and Zen tell us there is no death. Our life doesn't end with our skin. *Ku* and *shiki* are not in two separate places: *ku* exists in *shiki* and *shiki* in *ku*. So, no death—in other words, no death of the mind. No birth, no death.

This being the case, you can understand the importance of the idea of karma in Buddhism, and the extreme freedom that is associated with it. In effect, because there is neither birth nor death, each of us, at any moment, can transform and cut our own karma.

Nihilists believe the opposite of this. By saying that nothing exists and that in the end there is only death—just one side—they deny the karmic consequences of their actions. But there can be no nihilism if we say that *ku* "in and of itself" (*sokuze*) is *shiki*, and that *shiki* "in and of itself" is *ku*: A *ku identical to both includes all phenomena*. Then subject and object are one and the same *ku*; and when subject and object become one, Sosan tells us, everything is included.

To put it another way, when you lose the particular—the self, the subject/object duality—you obtain the whole, the totality. This is the loss we experience directly during zazen.

Zazen means losing something. Things are taken away from you, removed. Zazen after zazen, all the useless baggage you've been carrying around with you is set down. And after years of practice you realize that by losing yourself, you receive everything. Because then you find your true nature, which is always different from one person to the next.

145

When the monk Dogen returned from China after having studied for three years with Master Nyojo, the committee of officials who met him when he got off the boat asked him, "What have you brought back from China?"

"Empty-handed, I return with nothing."

And because they did not understand, he added,

"Eyes horizontal, nose vertical."

Sometimes people talk about zazen without knowing what it's really about; they say they don't want to lose their existence, their being. "In this mind—*ku*—not only can I not obtain anything, but what's worse, I'm going to lose myself. I won't be me anymore." They're afraid of what they'll find, afraid of this "everything." Often, they escape: they stop practicing zazen.

It's true, Soto Zen teaching and practice can be frightening: we're afraid of *ku*. People feel as though they're facing oblivion, on the edge of a precipice, and they're not ready for it. They want to go slowly, step by step; they want to climb the ladder progressively and not be catapulted all at once to the top of the mountain. Rinzai Zen, for example, sees the practice as a ladder to be climbed rung by rung, koan after koan (two thousand in all), after which you're at the top: it's the great awakening of Buddha. Personally, I've never practiced that way, and I have doubts as to the effectiveness of this method.

There's no reason to be afraid. Afraid of what? Afraid of losing your incompleteness? Afraid of dying? In the end, isn't that our practice: dying?

Going to sesshin is a good way to practice dying. Sesshin means taking away something special, taking away every idea, abandoning every thought—the negative and the positive. And abandoning your thoughts—that's "dying." Dying to yourself, to your own ideas. And in the final analysis, dying is very pleasant. At least during zazen.

As Master Deshimaru used to say all the time, "Zazen is getting into your coffin." Master Kodo Sawaki often spoke about the point of view of the coffin, too. He said, "Look at the world and yourself from the inside of your coffin and you will see that all the things you take so much to heart are not that important." This is especially true when you practice a sesshin exactly, following the teaching and the breathing. In daily life, however, we're very afraid to die, perhaps because we've lost contact with our true self. It's a question of faith. Without faith, our lives remain torn between contradictions. Practicing zazen, especially during a sesshin, means finding this true self, touching this true mind. Then, doubt and fear vanish, leaving room for faith without object, true faith. Faith in what? Faith in yourself? Who is that?

What's important is to understand, in your guts, what *ku* means, and to have faith in that, to practice the Way according to this teaching. Have faith in the fact that you are just a particle of *ku*, the emptiness from which all things come and to which all things continually return; and therefore you are unlimited.

Here's a poem written by a Buddhist monk named Jo Hoshi, who was executed in 414 for having refused to obey an order from the emperor. Jo Hoshi wrote this poem the morning of his execution:

> *Originally, the four elements have no master.*
> *The five skandha are essentially empty.*
> *I now place my head facing the sword:*
> *Let's do it like hoeing the spring breeze.*

30

Make no distinction between subtle and gross.
There are no sides to take.

This strophe describes the state of mind—the unconscious, automatic and natural state—of the man or woman of the Way. It's the unifying thread in the life of the sage and the artist.

Make no distinction between subtle and gross. Don't discriminate, don't choose: that's not complicated, and most of us have heard this teaching before. But putting it into practice is another thing entirely.

It means, for example, not making comparisons. Because when you compare yourself to other people or to yourself, you're only producing *subtle* or *gross.* People who have been practicing for many years are very familiar with this phenomenon.

The practice of zazen itself often becomes a means of discrimination. In the dojo, you look at another person out of the corner of your eye and think, "Oh, he's always moving, but I'm hanging in there"; or, "I'm better than her, my posture is better, my understanding is superior"; or the opposite: "I'm suffering like a dog and I can't help moving, while he isn't budging an inch!"

It's inevitable to react this way in the beginning; at that point, this type of discrimination can even help you. In the very beginning of my practice, for example, I couldn't accept the fact that everyone else could do zazen without moving, without any apparent difficulty, whereas I was having a lot of difficulty. Looking at the others, I judged myself inferior, and this comparison motivated me—even if it was a gross point of view.

And then, like many people, little by little I went from this gross discrimination to a refined, subtle discernment, in the sense that I no longer looked at other people much, but at myself instead. Observing yourself is a subtle practice. But this new way of seeing can also become a form of discrimination; because in looking at myself, I began to compare myself to me.

Many people suffer from this subtle discrimination, which is based on mistaken opinions. You often hear practitioners say, "In the beginning, I was progressing on the Way, I was improving, I was going somewhere. But not anymore. Now I have the impression that I'm stagnating, that I'm going backwards." So some people ask themselves, "Why aren't I progressing anymore? Am I observing myself correctly? Maybe I am progressing and don't know it? Or maybe I can't go beyond a certain level and I'm sliding back."

But what happens with years of practice—and on the condition, of course, that you practice regularly and correctly—is that you stop comparing yourself to your self (even if you continue to observe yourself). Because little by little and unconsciously, you understand *mushotoku*, "without object"; you don't fill your thoughts with a goal anymore—the one, for example, about becoming a better person; you're no longer preoccupied with the idea of awakening . . . and all the discriminations, all the comparisons fall away by themselves, unconsciously and automatically.

༜

Looking at yourself directly during zazen is not that difficult, but freeing yourself from your personal conditioning, your habits and your personal viewpoints is another matter.

So, *make no distinction between subtle and gross.* If you make no distinction between differences, judgments, opinions and values, you will be free from all constraints; you will no longer be tempted by your preconceived ideas, your prejudices, your erroneous opinions; you will simply stop choosing with your personal consciousness. But if you throw yourself into your thoughts all the time, you will be led to make endless choices, or, in Sosan's words, to always "take sides."

People often say, "If you don't have an opinion, if you haven't taken a side, then you're lost." But that's just conventional wisdom. "Ah, he's so intelligent! She's so beautiful!" Or even cruder: "He's such an asshole! She's such a dog!" On the contrary, do what Sosan says: stop discriminating between subtle and gross. He is. She is.

A field, seen from up close, is full of bumps; it's not completely even. But if you move away, it becomes infinitely flat, like a lawn. In the same way, you think one thing is profound and subtle, another thing simplistic and gross. You may acquire, say, a taste for oysters, and a disdain for meat and potatoes. But gross or subtle, in the end there's not much separating them.

"What nationality are you? How old are you? Are your parents still alive? Do they have money?" Are these questions gross or subtle? When a monk arrives at a monastery, the master doesn't ask these kinds questions. He says, "Hello! The pure wind caresses the spotless moon; the stream girds the mountain's waist."

The Way, like the field, does not change. It is always there, under your feet. It's just *you* changing, you and your illusory viewpoints, you who are endlessly torn between right and left, pulled by karma, continually slipping from gross into subtle and back again. Some of us spend our lives juggling our reflections on right and wrong and good and bad, always wanting explanations.

Ordinary people, driven by their karma, live in the world and also in time. They live in transmigration, the cycle of births and deaths, *samsara*. The advantage of becoming a monk or nun and practicing zazen is that you are directly confronted with your karma, and, through zazen, have the possibility to cut it and get out of transmigration.

Our job is to cut karma. When we're in zazen, we create very little karma, because we don't speak or move. The karma of the mouth and the body are momentarily suspended. In daily life, on the other hand, we never stop talking, and even if we don't really mean what we say, we say it anyway, and the karma of the mouth gets going.

Karma is typically human; so in order to not create karma during zazen, you have to follow the advice of Ota Roshi, one of Kodo Sawaki's disciples: "Do not bring anything human into the heart of zazen." To avoid initiating this karma of discrimination, he said, "simply cut off your head and place it next to you during zazen." Far from being harsh, these words reflect infinite compassion—a compassion which applies to all human beings, even though each one has his or her own characteristics.

For example, there are people who always think in terms of political or social events: they think about Christmas or the New Year; they think about a football game, the lottery, the holidays. Others think only in terms of judgment: they spend their time criticizing, finding other people worthless. Still others think exclusively about their family, their wife, their husband, their friends—I know a woman who only thinks about her boss. Some only think about sex, others about food, or clothes—they're always asking themselves what they're going to wear today—leather pants? jeans? pimp shoes? cowboy boots? And then there are those who only think about themselves: "What do these people think of me?" "Those people don't like me!" "Do they find me attractive?" "Was my lecture good?" "Is this teaching okay?"

All these states of mind resemble each other very closely; it's always a matter of discriminating points of view belonging to people who have completely "taken sides." These people believe themselves to be in the normal condition, but that's not the case at all.

Another way of discriminating is the one that consists of always thinking about the future—"With all the money I'm going to win in the lottery, I'll be able to have a lot of fun!"—or endlessly projecting into the past—"Why did I waste all my money on that stupid lottery ticket?"—which amounts to the same thing.

One of the most common characteristics of human beings is always being caught up in the past, always wanting to go back there, so much so that we're never in the present moment, and our aspiration to the Way dries up. This is why zazen is absolutely indispensable: to understand in your guts that it is the path itself, here and now, that is important.

When he was dying of cancer, Zen master Reikai Vendetti described how he had learned to "get out of the past and jump with both feet into the here and now"—and I suppose he did it

151

through the practice of zazen. He also said that he asked himself, "Why was I born? Why am I going to die?" Now those are some important questions! "But now," he added, "it seems much more important to me to be in the present, to follow the present moment."[15]

❧

No longer picking, choosing or discriminating, no longer thinking about the past or the future, no longer feeding those ideas of "who am I?"—Buddhism teaches us that this is what the practice leads us to in the end, and that with time all these reflections fall away, and there is evolution and transformation. *Shiki sokuze ku, ku sokuze shiki*: non-form becomes form or phenomena, and vice versa. And it's not a closed circle in which you go from *ku* to *shiki* and from *shiki* to *ku*. It's not a simple symmetrical relationship between *ku* and *shiki*, but an evolution: *ku* is developed and transformed; it grows and expands.

You understand through your body, you understand *ku*, which is nothing other than yourself. And the question "Who am I?" falls away all by itself. You're no longer interested in your little being. With the practice, you even begin to understand the other person's point of view, and to embrace it unconsciously.

I think this understanding is absolutely necessary. Obviously, it has nothing to do with psychology or those little manuals about "How to Behave," "How to Make Friends" or "How to Be Loved." Understanding others doesn't mean making friends in the sangha, getting close and seeing each other all the time.

Remember Master Fuyodokai, who said, "Don't spend your daily life for your own benefit, don't just be interested in your own health. Cut off both heads, and the one in the middle as well." Which means, don't love this, don't detest that. It's true, we often go towards what we consider to be good for us, while fleeing from what we judge to be bad. Don't look for what is good, beautiful and

---

[15] Reikai Vendetti and Luc Boussard, *Pèlerinage chez les maîtres éminents* (*Pilgrimage to Eminent Masters*) (Paris: Editions Sully, 1999), pp. 137-9.

profound; don't run away from what is stupid and ugly. Don't love the right head and don't hate the left head. Same for the head in the middle.

The more you practice zazen, the less you follow your personal thoughts and the less you have these problems of choice. The more you practice, the less you worry about your little well-being.

For a long time, Vasubandhu, though he had many disciples, did not have the official transmission from his master. He ate only once a day, always before noon, always sat in meditation, never slept and never neglected to make offerings to Buddha day and night.

Yet he still did not have the *shiho*.

One day, Vasubandhu's disciples went to find Jayrata to talk to him about it. After explaining all of Vasubandhu's good actions and qualities—that he was pure, celibate and vegetarian, and that he was already famous and had many more disciples than Jayrata himself—they asked the old patriarch, "Why, under these conditions, do you not give him the *shiho*?"

Jayrata replied: "Your master is far from the Way. Even if he continues like this for many *kalpa*, it will always be a source of illusions."

"How can you say that about such a deserving master?" he disciples wanted to know, very surprised.

"I do not seek the Way," answered Jayrata, "and yet I am not plunged into error. I do not make offerings to the Buddha, nor do I hold him in contempt. I do not practice long hours of meditation, nor am I lazy. Without choosing, I eat what's in front of me. I am neither modest nor greedy. Wanting nothing at all: this is called the Way."

❧

Make no distinction between subtle and gross.
There are no sides to take.

If you can get the meaning of this strophe into your guts and understand it, not with your head, but through your body— through the *hara*, the *tanden*, and through zazen—you will never again be overwhelmed by attacks or criticism, you will never again be unhappy when faced with hate or scorn, nor happy, faced with love or veneration. These things will simply no longer touch you at all.

This is what Fuyodokai meant when he said, "Even if a voice or a color seduces you, you must be like someone planting flowers in stone. Even if you see honors arise, they are just dust to clear out of your eyes."

Be rootless. That's the meaning of the thirtieth strophe.

31

The substance of the great Way is generous.
It is neither hard nor easy.

The thirty-first strophe of the *Shinjinmei*, which is almost the center of the poem, is one of its most famous and most poetic verses.

The great Way is wide, vast, generous—*generous* meaning "cosmic," "unlimited."

We often hear that zazen is the door to the Way. But I don't think that's a very good image. The Way is big—so big, so wide, that it has no door. And there's no place where you could put one. Can there be a door to the cosmos? How could the Way have a door when it has no way in and no way out? What good would a door be, knowing that no one enters and no one leaves?

The great Way is the normal, original condition of the mind. How can you enter or leave the normal, original condition?

It's your face before the birth of your parents, before the birth of your grandparents and your great-grandparents, before the birth of Charlemagne, before the birth of the cavemen, before the birth of Adam and Eve. You may think you weren't there, but in that case, you wouldn't be here today. That's what *the great Way* means.

Generous also means "universal," "all-inclusive," "not limited."

The Way, especially the Way of Zen, is completely free. Many people picture it as a clearly marked path, like the jet trail of a Boeing, or the tracks of a train. They follow very strict rules and live like locomotives rather than sages.

The Way is not pinned down by any rule, or situated in any set place. In fact, it's not anywhere. You can't find the Way in a bookstore. You can't find it in a university. You can't find it in Goethe or Bukowski or Picasso. You can't find it in the artist's studio, or in books on Zen. Yet many people prefer to study Zen, to have contact with it through books, rather than to practice it.

Sekko was a painter in ancient China who adored painting paper dragons. He spent all his time talking about paper dragons and collecting them. A real dragon heard about Sekko and his paper imitations, and thought, "If a real dragon like me came to visit him, he could paint the real thing and he would be very happy." So the dragon went to see Sekko. But he was mistaken. When Sekko saw him—"AAAAAAAH!"—it was a terrible shock.

The phenomenal world is not reality. Reality is simply here, now. This is what you confirm during zazen by continually coming back to your posture and breathing. In order to come back to your own body—which is not really yours—it's important not to follow your thoughts.

Presence is what's real, not the phenomenal aspect of the body. Universal, original nature constitutes reality. That's why it's not necessary to be an admirer of dragons—or of monks. Be the dragon itself, and you will never again be frightened by one.

This is how the great Way is vast, generous, universal, cosmic, free, unlimited. here are so many words, because the Way is everywhere, not just in the dojo; because it includes existence and non-existence (*shiki* and *ku*); because it is everything, and it is nowhere.

So don't look for it. You're wasting your time. It's like looking for air.

༺❀༻

The substance of the great Way is generous.
It is neither easy nor hard.

The thirty-first strophe echoes the first strophe in the *Shinjinmei*:

Practicing the Way is not difficult,
But you must not love, or hate, or choose, or reject.

In this poem, Sosan often comes back to the question of choice. Choosing makes life difficult, though it's not always easy to avoid selecting or choosing. We're always taking sides, defending personal viewpoints on one subject or another. But these kinds of discussions limit life. They do absolutely nothing to create an *i shin den shin* connection: heart-to-heart communication.

One day a monk asked Master Deshimaru to talk to him about space. "Everything exists in space," said the master, "but where does space exist?" The monk could not reply. The master said that these kinds of questions are pointless. They are concerned with division or quantity, and in fact only hinder us.

The same goes for another question that many people used to ask themselves about Master Deshimaru: Was he an authentic master or not? "He can't be a master—he drinks," said some. Others said, "Sure, he's a master—at least when he's in the dojo." Still others wondered, "But is he really *my* master? Wouldn't I be better off going somewhere else?" Since at the time there was nowhere else to go, these people stayed by him. But when he died, most of them left.

Always picking and choosing. Maybe it's normal, in the beginning; but later, if you practice sincerely, you don't think about those kinds of questions anymore: "Is he my master or not?"

For years now in the United States there's been some debate in Zen circles about whether or not to wear black robes, chant the sutras in English or in Sino-Japanese, wear the kesa or rakusu, or even receive the ordination. This debate has come to France, where an elder disciple of Master Deshimaru, who has become a fervent advocate of the Westernization of Zen practice, renounced his monk's ordination because of his ideas of what defines a monk. For example, "All monks have always lived in monasteries, and since I do not, I am not a monk." This person is forgetting that his own master, Deshimaru, never lived in a monastery, and that his master's master, Kodo Sawaki, was called "Homeless Kodo" because he traveled so extensively to teach the Dharma outside of the Japanese temple system.

When you pick and choose like this, the Way is not very generous, great, wide or vast. If, on the other hand, you stop choosing between this and that, then your doubts will disappear and true practice can begin: *funi*, not-two.

Because the Way in and of itself is neither hard nor easy. The practice is neither hard nor easy, even if you sometimes suffer during zazen.

Each of us carries our difficulty within us. Difficulty (or nondifficulty) is all in your head; it just depends on you and where you are. Things become hard or easy when, for example, you set yourself a goal on the Way, and you measure the distance that separates you from that goal: "I'm not ready yet. I'm practicing, but I'm not quite there yet."

One day, a young man who practiced *kendo* went to see a great master and asked to become his disciple. The master looked at him and said nothing. The young man was somewhat disconcerted, but he was very eager.

"How long do you think it will take for me to learn your technique?" he asked.

"Oh, about ten years," replied the master.

"Ten years! That's too long! If I train and work twice as hard as everyone else, how long will it take?"

"Thirty years," said the master.

"Oh, master, you're joking! I'll do anything to learn your *kendo* method, anything!"

"In that case," said the master, "it'll take you fifty years."

What is the goal? What distance separates you from it? Are there signs to show you the way?

No. There are no signs, nor is there any distance to cover or time to transcend. There is no goal, because you are the goal. Right where you're walking, right where you are: that's the goal, that's the Way. The Way has never changed. It's under your feet, and you cannot walk anywhere else.

"Where do you come from?" the master asks the monk who arrives at the monastery gate.

"I'm from Paris," or "I'm from Brooklyn," the monk generally replies.

And the master slams the door in his face.

This kind of exchange is quite common in Zen. It almost always takes the form of a mondo between two people: the disciple who is sincerely seeking the Way, and the master who wants to help her and always asks questions that bring her back to herself.

This teaching has always been protected and preserved—but not like preserves in a jar, which always end up going bad. You can't use other people's discoveries just as you find them, like taking a jar off a shelf. Times change, circumstances change, languages change. Master Kodo Sawaki took the expression of the Way out of the antiquated context it had fallen into and brought it into modernity. Master Deshimaru and others of his generation transplanted it into a Western context. And now it's up to us to make it understandable for today's generation.

From the beginning, it has been up to each of us constantly to rediscover this teaching, to make an effort again and again through an authentic practice, continually to embody the Way anew through the practice of zazen.

In his commentary on the *Shinjinmei*, Master Deshimaru says, "We must create our path. But the source, the origin, is unique: zazen."

In zazen, when your hands slide forward, you bring them back in against your abdomen. When your body slumps, you pull your thighs and waist upward, you stretch your spine and the back of your neck. That's zazen. Zazen is action—action in the present moment.

I think that's what Buddha was showing us, when he said that everyone could do what he did, everyone could become like him. In Zen you don't even have to believe in Buddha; simply believe that we are all Buddha, that today, here and now, we all have the possibility to become men and women of satori, men and women who are fully awakened.

So in the end, why not be calm? Why not be free? That's *the substance of the great Way—do*—which is neither easy nor hard, but consists simply of knowing how to be awakened in your everyday life.

Author's Note

In addition to the translations of the *Shinjinmei* mentioned in the text, the following books were essential in my study of the poem:

Deshimaru, Taisen. *The Voice of the Valley: Zen Teachings.* Ed. Philippe Coupey. Indianapolis and New York: Bobbs-Merrill, 1979.

_____. *Sit: Zen Teachings of Master Taisen Deshimaru.* Ed. Philippe Coupey. Prescott, AZ: Hohm Press, 1996.

_____. *Shinjinmei.* 2 vols. Paris: Association Zen Internationale, 1990.

_____. *Shobogenzo: Introduction et commentaires.* Paris: Le Courrier du livre, 1970.

Sawaki, Kodo. *Le Chant de l'Eveil: Le Shodoka commenté par un maître zen.* Paris: Albin Michel, 1999.

Glossary

Amida Buddha (Skt., Amitabha), lit. "Endless Light." Mahayana Buddha embodying wisdom and mercy; venerated by the Pure Land School of Chinese and Japanese Buddhism, in the belief that simply invoking this name can lead to rebirth in paradise. See also *nembutsu*.

Asura. See *samsara*.

Atman. Hindu term for the soul or immortal quality of human beings. The existence of an *atman* is denied in Buddhism, which teaches that all phenomena are empty. See also *skandha*.

Avatamsaka Sutra, lit. "Sutra of the Buddhas' Garland." Mahayana sutra which became very important in China, in the various Ch'an schools as well as the Hua-yen (Jap., Kegon) School. It teaches that the human mind is the cosmos itself, and that Buddha, mind and all beings are one. The sutra exists only in Tibetan and Chinese translations; the oldest Chinese translation dates from the fifth century.

Baso Doitsu (Ch., Ma-tsu Tao-i, 709-788). Disciple of Nangaku and master of Hyakujo, Nansen, Daibai Hojo and layman P"ang; patriarch of Rinzai Zen known for his intense training methods, including shouts, gestures and blows with a stick, designed to jolt disciples out of their everyday thinking and into enlightenment. See also *Sekito Kisen*.

Bodaishin, lit. "mind of awakening." The mind that aspires to the Way, to the highest dimension; the mind that observes *mujo*, impermanence.

Bodhidharma (Jap., Bodaidaruma or Daruma, 470-543?). Disciple of Indian master Prajnadhara (Jap., Hannyatara) and master of Eka; first Chinese Zen patriarch and twenty-eighth after Shakyamuni Buddha in the Indian lineage. The son of a Brahmin king, he spent the last decade of his life in China. When he arrived there, he occupied a cave on the site of the Shorinji Monastery

(Ch., Shao-lin) on Mount Suzan (Ch., Sung-shan), where he sat facing the wall for nine years.

Bodhisattva. Human or celestial being who incarnates the Mahayana ideal. Contrary to the *arhat* in Hinayana Buddhism, who dedicates himself exclusively to his personal salvation, the bodhisattva vows to put aside his own liberation and be reborn until all beings are saved. See *shiguseiganmon.*

Bodhi tree. Fig tree (*ficus religiosa*) under which Shakyamuni Buddha had the experience of awakening after forty-nine days of zazen.

Bonno. Illusion; attachment; a product of personal consciousness. The vow to cut *bonnos* is one of the four great vows of the bodhisattva. See *shiguseiganmon.*

Bovay, Missen Michel (b. 1944). Zen master, close disciple of Master Taisen Deshimaru; former president of the International Zen Association in Europe; currently head of the Zurich Zen Dojo in Switzerland; received Dharma transmission from Okamoto Roshi in 1998.

Budo, lit. "the way of the warrior." Term designating the traditional Japanese martial arts.

Chikuso. See *samsara.*

Daibai Hojo (Ch., Ta-mei Fa-ch'ang, 752-839). Disciple of Baso and master of Koshu Tenryu. After thirty years of Buddhist book-learning, he met Baso, became his disciple and received his transmission. Then he left to practice zazen alone in the mountains for thirty years before accepting disciples of his own.

Daichi Sokei (1290-1366). Japanese Zen master famous for his poetry. He became a monk under Kangan Gin (1217-1300), a disciple of Dogen, and later practiced with Keizan for seven years. At age twenty-five he went to China, where he remained for eleven years. When he returned to Japan, he received the transmission from Meiho Sotetsu (1277-1350), a close disciple of Keizan.

Daikaku (posthumous name of Rankei Doryu, Ch., Lan-ch'i Tao-lung, 1213-1278). Chinese master and calligrapher of the Rinzai School; studied with many Chinese masters, most notably Wu-chun Shih-fan (Jap., Bushun Shiban); traveled to Japan in 1246, where he founded the Kenchoji Monastery in Kamakura in 1253.

Danken. Nihilism; theory which propounds the non-existence of any dimension other than the phenomenal world; the belief that existence ends with death. See *joken.*

Deshimaru, Taisen (1914-1982). Disciple of Kodo Sawaki; Japanese master of Soto Zen who spent the last fifteen years of his life teaching in Europe. Received monastic ordination, as well as the robe, bowl and spiritual transmission, from Kodo Sawaki in 1965. Founded more than a hundred dojos in Europe, North Africa and Canada, as well as La Gendronnière Temple in France's Loire Valley. According to temple records, he ordained more than five hundred monks and nuns, and more than twenty thousand people practiced with him at one time or another.

Deva. See *samsara.*

Dharma. 1) the universal truth, teaching and Buddhist doctrine pronounced by Shakyamuni Buddha; 2) the truth, ultimate reality or universal order; 3) phenomena, or manifestations of reality.

Diamond Sutra (Skt., Vajrachchedika-parjnaparamita-sutra). Independent section of the *Prajnaparamita Sutra,* which took on considerable importance, principally in the countries of Southeast Asia; explains that phenomena are not reality, but merely illusions, projections of our own minds.

Do (Ch., Tao or Dao). The Way; in Zen, the Buddha-Dharma.

Dogen Zenji (1200-1253). Disciple of Chinese master Nyojo and master of Ejo; introduced Soto Zen to Japan and founded Eiheiji Temple in the northern mountains of Japan. Born into a noble family, he studied Rinzai Zen and the koan method for several years with masters Eisai and Myozen, then crossed the sea to China where he met Soto master Nyojo. He practiced with Nyojo on Mount Tendo for three years before returning to Japan as the heir of Nyojo's Zen. His masterwork is the *Shobogenzo*, which contains the major part of his teaching. His poems are collected in the *Sanshodoei*, with the exception of the *Eiheikoroku* poems, which were reserved for his closest disciples and kept secret for many years.

Dojo. In Zen and the martial arts, a place to practice the Way.

Doshin (Ch., Tao-hsin, 580-651). Fourth Ch'an patriarch, disciple of Sosan and master of Konin; created a community of five hundred disciples on Mount Shuang-feng, where he died in zazen.

Doshu. How each person communicates the Way; expression of the Way through the body, speech, awareness and behavior; expression of the self, of one's awakening and one's understanding of the Dharma.

Eiheikoroku. Ten-volume collection of Master Dogen's sayings and poems; represents Dogen's teaching, as recorded by his direct disciples, from the time of his occupation of Koshoji Temple until his death.

Eisai Zenji (also Myoan Eisai or Senko Kokushi, 1141-1215). Japanese master of the Rinzai lineage, disciple of Hsu-an Huai-ch'ang (Jap., Kian Esho) and Dogen's master before Nyojo; founder of Shofukuji, the first monastery in Japan in which Rinzai Zen was practiced.

Eka (Ch., Hui-k'o, 487-593). Second Zen patriarch, disciple of Bodhidharma and master of Sosan; reported to have cut off his left arm to present to his master as a sign of his earnest desire to study the Dharma. He remained with Bodhidharma for nine years, practicing only *shikantaza*. After receiving the transmission, he went to live in the city, where he worked as a street sweeper and spread the Dharma.

Engaku. Level of buddha-for-self; someone who practices in order to be in good health and become a saint. See *pratyeka buddha*.

Engo Kokugon (Ch., Yuan-wu K'o-ch'in, 1063-1135). Chinese Rinzai master, disciple of Goso Hoen and master of Gokoku Keigen, Kukyu Joryu and Daie Soko; editor of the *Pi-yen-lu*, one of the best-known collections of koans.

Eno (Ch., Hui-neng, 638-713). Disciple of Konin and master of Seigen Gyoshi and Nangaku Ejo; author of *The Platform Sutra*. He arrived at Konin's temple on Mount Obai when he was twenty-four and left after only six months. For fifteen years he lived with fishermen and hunters, then taught the Dharma on Mount Sokei for thirty-six years until his death.

Fukanzazengi, lit. "General Presentation of the Principles of Zazen." Written by Master Dogen in 1227, soon after his return from China. This text, which cites the *Shinjinmei*, emphasizes the fact that zazen, far from constituting "a means to achieve enlightenment," is the fundamental practice of all buddhas.

Fuke (Ch., P'u-hua, d. 860). Chinese Zen master, disciple of Banzan Hoshaku; known for his eccentric behavior; friend of Master Rinzai and his disciples, with whom he played the role of a "holy fool."

Funi, lit. "not-two." The non-dualistic quality of reality.

Fuyodokai (Ch., Fu-jung Tao-kai, 1043-1118). Zen master in the Soto lineage; master of Tanka Shijun; highly respected in Zen for having restored the original purity of the practice while avoiding the two major pitfalls of the time: the intellectualism of the Soto School's *go i* (lit. "five degrees of enlightenment") and the theatricality of the Rinzai School's koans.

Gaitan. Corridor at the entrance of a dojo; reserved for kitchen staff who must leave the dojo during zazen, as well as anyone who is sick, tends to move, or might in any way disturb the atmosphere of the dojo.

Gassho. Joining both hands at nose-level, forearms horizontal, and bowing forward from the waist; ancient universal gesture expressing veneration, humility and respect, as well as the unity of body and mind: *funi*, non-duality.

Gendronnière (La). Zen temple located in France's Loire Valley, founded by Master Taisen Deshimaru in 1979; main temple of the sangha of Master Deshimaru's disciples, recognized by the Japanese Soto Zen authorities and regrouping over two hundred Zen dojos and groups worldwide. In 1984, Niwa Zenji came to La Gendronnière to give Dharma transmission to three of Master Deshimaru's disciples. In addition to a two-month summer retreat and intensive sesshin in winter, spring and fall, the temple hosts workshops, symposia, conferences and other activities focusing on Zen Buddhism. Above all, it is a practice center dedicated to sesshin, daily zazen and *samu*.

Genjokoan, lit. "Accomplished Koan" or "Accomplished Law." *Shobogenzo* chapter placed by Dogen at the beginning of the seventy-five-volume edition; undoubtedly the chapter most often translated, cited and commented on, despite its difficulty and density; deals essentially with the relationship between practice and enlightenment; includes the well-known parables of the moon and its reflection, wood and ashes, the bird and the fish, and the famous maxim, "Studying the Way is studying oneself..."

Genmai. Rice soup eaten after morning zazen while chanting the *Gyohatsunenju* (Meal Sutra).

Genpo Merzel (b. 1944). Contemporary American Zen master, disciple of Taizan Maezumi Roshi, from whom he received Dharma transmission in 1980; follower of the Sanbo Kyodan School, a mixed form of Rinzai and Soto Zen developed by Haku'un Yasutani and Daiun Sogaku Harada.

Gozu (Ch., Niu-t'ou, also known as Hoyu, Ch., Fa-jung, 594-657). Disciple of Doshin, co-disciple of Konin; created his own branch of Zen—"Gozu Zen"—which continued to be taught for a century after his death, then died out; author of "The Mind's Chant," a long poem similar to the *Shinjinmei*.

Gutei (Ch., Chu-chih, ninth century). Disciple of Koshu Tenryu, from whom he inherited "raised-thumb Zen," which he taught all his life.

Gyoji, lit. *gyo*, practice, action, behavior; *ji*, to maintain, to keep. Continuous or eternal practice, without beginning or end; the uninterrupted sequence of meditation and activity; title of a *Shobogenzo* chapter in which Dogen uses the history of the patriarchs to teach correct behavior.

Hakuin Ekaku (1689-1769). One of the most important masters in the Rinzai School; reaffirmed the importance of zazen, which this school had neglected in favor of intellectual text study; well versed in the koan system, he created a new presentation of it which is still used in Rinzai; he was also an accomplished painter, calligrapher and writer.

Hannya Shingyo. Abbreviated name of the *Maka Hannyaharamita Shingyo*, or *Heart Sutra*, chanted every morning after zazen in all Zen temples. This short sutra formulates the "heart" or essence of the Mahayana teaching on *ku* (emptiness).

Hannyatara (Skt., Prajnadhara). Twenty-seventh patriarch in the Indian Ch'an lineage; master of Bodhidharma.

Hara (also known as *kikai tanden*). Vital-energy center located just under the navel, which connects human beings to the cosmos. In Zen and the martial arts, energy which is free from tension and personal will is expressed through the *hara*.

Hekiganroku (Ch., Pi-yen-lu), lit. "The Blue-Green Cliff Record." Oldest collection of koans, written in the twelfth century by Ch'an master Yuan-wu K'o-ch'in (Jap., Engo

Kokugon). Valued for the important teachings and anecdotes it contains, this text is also considered a masterwork of classical Chinese poetry.

Hinayana (also known as Theravada), lit. "Small Vehicle," as opposed to Mahayana, "Great Vehicle." Ancient Buddhism which developed between the Buddha's death and the end of the first century BCE; presents a doctrine of salvation, the quest for nirvana through retreating from the world, and respect for monastic rules; implanted mainly in southern Asia (Ceylon, Thailand, Burma, Cambodia and Laos).

Hishiryo, lit. *hi*, beyond; *shiryo*, thinking. Thinking from the depths of not-thinking, beyond personal consciousness. This term, which in fact contains the secret, inexpressible essence of Zen, appears for the first time in the *Shinjinmei*. It is also found in a famous mondo between Master Yakusan and a monk ("How does one think without thinking?" asks the monk. "*Hishiryo*," replies Yakusan.), and in the teaching of Master Dogen. Along with *shikantaza* and *mushotoku*, *hishiryo* is one of the three pillars of the teaching of masters Kodo Sawaki and Taisen Deshimaru.

Hokyozanmai (Ch., San-mei-k'o), lit. "Samadhi of the Precious Mirror." Poem composed in the ninth century by Tozan Ryokai which celebrates the true nature of all things; recited every day in Japanese Zen temples; considered to be one of the founding texts of Soto Zen, along with the *Shinjinmei*, *Shodoka* and *Sandokai*.

Hotei (Ch., Pu-tai, d. 916). Chinese monk whose name means "sack of hemp," as he always carried one on his back. According to legend, his true identity was revealed upon his death: he was an avatar or incognito incarnation of Maitreya, the Buddha of the future. The image which remains of him is that of the Laughing Buddha, as represented in numerous statues in Chinese monasteries.

Hotetsu (Mayoku) (Ch., Ma-ku Pao-che, eighth-ninth centuries). Ch'an master, disciple of Baso Doitsu. Famous for his mondo about the fan.

Ikkyu Sojun (1394-1481). Rinzai master, poet and calligrapher, known for his eccentricity and iconoclasm. He called himself "Crazy Cloud" or "Blind Donkey," and claimed to prefer taverns and brothels to monasteries. In 1474 he was appointed abbot of Daitokuji, the temple where he had practiced for ten years in his youth before opting for a life outside of monasteries. He took great care not to name any successors.

Inmo, lit. "this," "that" or "thus." In Buddhism, reality "as it is," "thusness," the evident and indescribable character of things; term often used by Master Dogen, including as a title for one of the chapters of his *Shobogenzo*. In modern times, Professor D. T. Suzuki uses the word "suchness." Master Deshimaru did not use "suchness," and almost never *inmo*. He sometimes used the Japanese term *nyo* ("true freedom"), often repeating it—*nyo nyo*—and translating it as "infinite" or "eternal." But most of the time he simply used the English word "free."

Ippen (1239-1289). Wandering monk, founder of the Ji-shu School of Pure Land Buddhism. He believed that faith was an act of the mind and therefore subject to corruption. Consequently, he taught complete abandoning of the self, that is, of all mental attitudes, all attempts at understanding, and finally all religious realization: simply reject everything and invoke the *nembutsu*.

Isan Reiyu (Ch., Kuei-shan Ling-yu, 771-853). Disciple of Hyakujo, co-disciple of Obaku. He met his master when he was twenty-two, and served as tenzo in his monastery for twenty years before going off to found a temple in the mountains. He built a hut and remained in solitude for seven or eight years until a large number of disciples gathered around him, including Kyogen and Kyosan. The latter founded, with Isan, the Igyo School of Zen. Isan died in zazen posture.

I shin den shin, lit. "from mind to mind" or "from heart to heart." A fundamental notion in Zen which describes the transmission beyond writing and intellectual understanding, the common intuition between master and disciple of reality as it is.

Jayrata (Jap., Shayata, fourth century). Twentieth patriarch in the Indian Zen lineage, disciple of Kumaralata and master of Vasubandhu.

Jinshu (Ch., Shen-hsiu, 605-706). Disciple of Konin and co-disciple of Eno; founder of the Northern School of Ch'an, which advocated a gradual approach to the practice, and which survived for only a few generations after his death.

Jiun Sonja (1718-1804). Japanese master of the Shingon School, Sanskrit specialist and celebrated calligrapher. One day, his mother asked him to stop giving lectures, reproaching him for becoming a connoisseur of Buddhism. She advised him to settle down in a small, isolated temple and to devote his time to meditation.

Joken. Theory which propounds the eternal nature of the world and the self. See also *danken*.

Joshu Jushin (Ch., Chao-chou Ts'ung-shen, 778-897). One of the greatest Ch'an masters, disciple of Nansen, whom he followed for more than forty years. After his master's death, he set out wandering to deepen his Dharma experience with other Ch'an masters, finally settling in a small monastery where he became a master in his own right at the age of eighty. He had thirteen Dharma successors, yet his lineage died out after a few generations.

Joza. Term used in the seventh and eighth centuries when speaking to a co-disciple; equivalent of "monk" or "friend."

Kai. Precept. In Zen, the ten *kai* are the rules of natural morality which the disciple accepts from the master during the bodhisattva and monastic ordinations.

Kakunen musho, lit. "infinite sky, nothing sacred." When the Indian master Bodhidharma arrived in China, the emperor asked, "What is the sacred truth?" "*Kakunen musho*" was his reply.

Kalpa. Cosmic cycle; an infinitely long period of time.

Kan. Great vow made by all buddhas and bodhisattvas; profound aspiration to practice the Way and go beyond oneself.

Kanbun. Hybrid of classical Chinese and Japanese used in formal writings through World War II.

Kanji. Written Japanese alphabet of pictograms representing words or ideas, as opposed to *kana*, which represent syllables.

Karma. Law of cause and effect; the logical sequence of human behavior (thoughts, words and actions) and its good and bad consequences. Karma encourages correct behavior through the awareness of the effects of our comportment on the phenomenal world, rather than by following "commandments" or awaiting reward or retribution in heaven or hell. Both individual and collective karma exist, and both transcend birth and death. Each person's practice influences the karma of humanity as a whole.

Kassan Zen'e (Ch., Chia-shan Shank-hui 805-881). Disciple of ferryman-master Sensu Tokujo; an exemplary tenzo under several different masters; appears in Dogen's *Mountains and Rivers Sutra* and *Eiheikoroku*.

Katagiri, Dainin (1928-1990). Zen master, student of Eko Hashimoto in Japan and assistant to Shunryu Suzuki in the United States; founder of the Minnesota Zen Center.

Keizan Jokin (1268-1325). Considered the most important Japanese Soto Zen master after Dogen; practiced under the direction of Ejo and Gikai (two of Master Dogen's closest disciples); founder of Sojiji, one of the two principal Soto temples in Japan, along with Eiheiji; author of the *Denkoroku*, a collection of accounts of the Dharma transmission from Shakyamuni Buddha to Eihei Dogen.

Kendo, lit. "the Way of the sword." The art of Japanese samurai swordsmanship.

Kennett, Jiyu (1924-1996). English-born Soto master; studied Theravada Buddhism and Rinzai Zen before receiving Dharma transmission in 1963 from Keido Chisan Koho at Daihonzan Sojiji. She founded Shasta Abbey in California and several other temples and meditation groups in North America and Europe, and was also the founder of the Order of Buddhist Contemplatives.

Kesa. Large garment made of many pieces of cloth carefully stitched together, which monks and nuns wear draped around their shoulders over their kolomos. Presented by the master to the disciple during the ordination ceremony, the kesa is an object of faith and veneration. It symbolizes the transmission of and adherence to the uninterrupted line of Buddha's disciples, and existence in a dimension which transcends the small ego.

Ketsumyaku. Certificate given by the master to the disciple during ordinations; represents the lineage of masters who connect the newly ordained person to Shakyamuni Buddha.

Ki (Ch., *chi*). Vital energy or activity that animates all creatures; resides in the *hara* and is cosmic in nature; a key concept in Taoism and traditional Chinese medicine.

Kinhin. Slow walking meditation to the rhythm of one's breathing, practiced during the interval between two zazens.

Koan. Originally, in China, a law or judgment handed down from public authorities; in Zen, a universal truth expressed by a phrase from a sutra or a master; a paradox that only intuition can resolve, which steadfastly defies logical analysis; used as part of formal education in Rinzai Zen as a means to push disciples past their limits and into enlightenment. Soto Zen, which places no value on special states and considers satori the normal condition, generally does not use koans in the formal sense in disciple training. Nevertheless, for both Rinzai and Soto, the koan represents the hidden, ungraspable aspect of reality.

Kolomo. Long black robe with large sleeves worn by Zen monks and nuns, usually over a white or grey kimono.

Konin (Ch., Hung-jen, 601-674). Disciple of Doshin and master of Jinshu and Eno, who founded the Northern and Southern schools of Ch'an, respectively. All existing branches of Zen came from the Southern School. Konin met his master when he was fourteen and immediately impressed him with his profound understanding. After Doshin's death, he founded a monastery on Mount Obai.

Koshoji. Kyoto monastery where Dogen lived for ten years before founding Eiheiji. Here he formed his first community of monks according to the model he had experienced with Nyojo in China. It is also where he wrote most of the *Shobogenzo*, and where he met Ejo, who would become his successor.

Ku (Skt., *sunyata*). Often translated as "emptiness" or "void," as opposed to *shiki*, "phenomena." But the term should not be seen as expressing a nihilistic view of the world. It means infinity, the unborn from which all things born and finite come, and to which they return. It is the origin, the common identity without which differences (phenomena) could not exist.

Kusen. Oral teaching given during zazen; an *i shin den shin* teaching which is addressed directly to the listeners' *hishiryo*-consciousness, without passing through the intellect. Kusen appears to be a specificity of the Kodo Sawaki/Taisen Deshimaru lineage: most other lineages prefer lectures (*teisho*).

Kyogen Chikan (Ch., Hsiang-yen Chih-hsien, d. 898). Disciple of Isan Reiyu; an intellectual and great scholar who studied with Hyakujo but did not succeed in intimately understanding the essence of Zen. When Hyakujo died, Kyogen followed his co-disciple, Isan, with whom he came to full awakening.

Kyosaku, lit. "wake-up stick." Used during zazen to hit the trapezius muscles of practitioners disturbed by drowsiness or mental agitation. The *kyosaku* is not a form of punishment but a way to help restore the normal condition.

Maezumi, Hakuyu Taizan (1931-1995). Soto-Rinzai master certified by Hakujun Kuroda, Koryu Osaka and Hakuun Yasutani, making him a successor in three Zen lineages; founder of the Los Angeles Zen Center, the White Plum Asanga and several temples in the United States and Europe; certified a dozen disciples.

Mahakashyapa (sixth century BCE). One of the principal disciples of Shakyamuni Buddha; known for his self-discipline and moral strictness; assumed leadership of the sangha after Buddha's death; considered the first Zen patriarch.

Mahayana, lit. "Great Vehicle." Branch of Buddhism which includes Zen, popular primarily in Tibet, China, Korea and Japan. Its ideal—to save all beings rather than seeking individual salvation—is incarnated by the bodhisattva.

Mantra. In Hinduism and yoga, a sacred phrase given by the guru to the disciple, which encompasses the very essence of the divinity to which the teacher is dedicated; in Buddhism, a short invocation, usually taken from a sutra, whose sound, charged with energy (*ki*), carries a spiritual virtue or protective power. Mantras play an especially important role in Amidism (*nembutsu*) and Tibetan Buddhism.

Marpa (1012-1097). Celebrated yogi of Tibet, also called "the Translator"; disciple of Naropa and master of Milarepa; studied with Naropa in India for sixteen years before returning to his homeland to translate the sacred texts into Tibetan.

Menzan Zuiho (1683-1769). Zen master and celebrated Soto scholar; author of more than fifty works, including biographies of Master Dogen and commentaries on his teaching; sought to return the Soto temples of his time to the more orthodox ways of Dogen, an influence which continues in Japan to this day.

Milarepa (1025-1135). Considered the greatest saint of Tibet; disciple of the yogi Marpa, from whom he learned the *mahamudra*—freedom from emptiness and *samsara*.

Mondo, lit. "question/answer." Any form of exchange whose purpose is an attempt to understand the Dharma. When conducted in a dojo, mondos provide an opportunity for matters germane to existence and the practice to be clarified, not in the intimacy of private master-disciple interviews (*dokusan*), but for the benefit of the entire sangha. Many mondos have become part of Zen history for the edification of generations of disciples.

Morimoto, Kazuo (b.?). Disciple of Taisen Deshimaru; translator and professor at the Institute of Oriental Culture, Tokyo University; author of *From Derrida to Dogen: Deconstruction and the Cancellation of Body and Mind* (Fukuatke Books, 1989).

Mu. Particle meaning "nothing," "nothingness," or "no." Connotes absence rather than negation; found in Japanese expressions such as *mushotoku* ("non-profit"), *mushin* ("no-mind") and *muga* ("non-ego"); figures in the first koan in the *Mumonkan* (a monk asks Master Joshu, "Does a dog have Buddha-nature?" "*Mu*," replies Joshu).

Mujo (Skt., *anitya*). Impermanence; one of the three characteristics of existence, which gives rise to the other two: suffering (*duhkha*) and impersonality (*anatman*); the fundamental condition of all life. The study of *mujo* is an essential part of practicing the Way. Master Daichi wrote, "*Mujo* always lies in wait, at every moment, and when it strikes, it strikes with such speed and brutality that you are thunderstruck before you know what hit you."

Mumon Ekai (Ch., Wu-men Hui-k'ai, 1183-1260). Rinzai master, disciple of Gatsurin Shikan and master of Shinchi Kakushin; best known for his koan compilation, the *Mumonkan*.

Mumonkan (Ch., *Wu-men-kuan*), lit. "The Gateless Gate." Volume of forty-eight koans collected and commented on by Mumon Ekai in 1229.

Mushin, lit. "no-mind." No personal mind; no-thought; freedom from dualistic thinking.

Mushotoku, lit. "non-profit." No merit; nothing to obtain; refers to practicing without object or goal; giving freely. Master Deshimaru said it was the fundamental Zen teaching that brought him to the practice.

Nagarjuna (second-third centuries). Indian Buddhist philosopher, founder of the Madhyamika School (also known as "The Middle Path") and fourteenth patriarch after Buddha; known for his teachings on the doctrine of *ku* (Skt., *sunyata*, "emptiness"), which earned him the name "Father of Mahayana." His principal works are the *Madhyamaka-karika* and the *Mahaprajnaparamita Shastra*. Shortly before the end of his life, he burned all his books and sutras and consecrated himself exclusively to the study of the kesa.

Nansen Fugan (Ch., Nan-ch'uan P'u-yuan, 748-835). Disciple of Baso Doitsu and master of Joshu Jushin, among others. Seven years after his master's death, he went into isolation on Mount Nansen, where he practiced zazen for thirty years. Then he spent the last ten years of his life in a monastery, surrounded by more than a hundred disciples.

Naraka. See *samsara*.

Nembutsu. Recitation of the name of Amida Buddha. In Amidism, the fervent recitation of the phrase *Namu amida Butsu* ("praised be Amida Buddha") is believed to lead to rebirth in the heaven of the Pure Land. See also *Shin School*.

Nirvana. 1) definitive freedom from *samsara* (rebirth); 2) extinction of all desires and attachments; 3) the deepest *samadhi* in which consciousness is no longer tempted by illusions. In Zen, nirvana and *samsara* are identical in the eyes of someone who has penetrated the true nature of things, which is *ku* (emptiness).

Nirvana School. Lineage of Chinese Buddhism which appeared in the fifth century; devoted to the *Mahaparinirvana Sutra*; holds that all beings have Buddha-nature and that anyone can access Buddhahood through sudden enlightenment.

Noumenon (Skt., *svabhava*), lit. "self-nature." Lasting substance; independent existence.

Nyojo (Tendo) (Ch., T'ien-t'ung Ju-ching, 1163-1228). Ch'an master of the Soto School, disciple of Shingetsu Shoryo and master of Dogen Zenji; traveled from dojo to dojo, coming into contact with all types of Zen existing in his time: some mixed zazen with Taoism, Confucianism and the recitation of the *nembutsu*, others with koan study. Rejecting them all, he became abbot of Tendo Monastery in Southern China and taught only zazen.

Nyorai (Skt., *Tathagata*). 1) being who has arrived at supreme enlightenment; 2) the cosmic principle, the essence of the universe, the absolute.

Obaku Kiun (Ch., Huang-po Hsi-yun, d. 850). Ch'an master, disciple of Hyakujo Ekai and master of Rinzai Gigen and twelve others; known as a stately man of pure and simple character. The prime minister P'ei Hsiu became his disciple and had a monastery constructed where Obaku accepted to live.

Pratyeka buddha. A buddha-for-self; someone who practices to escape *samsara*, who has attained enlightenment by and for himself. See also *engaku*.

Preta. See *samsara*.

Rakusu. Small kesa worn around the neck, in the dojo and in daily life. As opposed to the kesa, the rakusu is not reserved for monks and nuns—everyone who has received the bodhisattva (lay) ordination receives and wears it.

Reikai Vendetti (d. 2001). Zen monk, disciple of Master Taisen Deshimaru; director of the Toulouse Dojo in France, he also led retreats in Corsica and Reunion Island; an accomplished painter whose work includes portraits of Buddhist masters (*Pilgrimage to Eminent Masters*, Editions Sully, 1999).

Reiun Shigon (Ch., Ling-yun Chih-ch'in, ninth century). Disciple of Isan Reiyu; author of "For thirty years I sought a master swordsman," this poem describing his satori:
How many times did the leaves fall
and the branches burst into bud?
But from the moment I saw the peach blossoms in flower,
From that time, I have had no doubts.

Rensaku. A series of blows administered by the master or an assistant with the *kyosaku* on the muscles situated between the shoulder and the neck; used when an error has been committed, to awaken the mind of the disciple, and also to awaken the concentration of the whole sangha.

Rinzai School. Lineage founded by Master Rinzai Gigen (d. 866), whose origin dates back to seventh-century master Nangaku Ejo, a disciple of Eno, as was Seigen Gyoshi, source of the Soto lineage; one of the two great branches of Zen still alive today, along with Soto; emphasizes obtaining satori and using koans as a meditation tool.

Ryutan (or Ryotan) **Soshin** (Ch., Lung-t'an Ch'ung-hsin, ninth century). Disciple of Tenno Dogo and master of Tokusan Senkan. He met his master in his childhood and regularly brought him rice cakes.

Samadhi (Jap., *zanmai*). State of meditation and open awareness during zazen; pure, unconscious concentration without object. Master Dogen said, "The *samadhi* of the buddhas and the patriarchs is frost and hail, wind and lightning."

Sampai. Three consecutive prosternations, with forehead touching the ground and hands raised to receive the Budda's feet.

Samsara. The cycle of existences (birth, death, rebirth) conditioned by attachment; opposite of nirvana; composed of six possible modes of existence: *shomon* (human), *asura* (warrior), *deva* (god), *chikuso* (animal), *preta* (hungry ghost), *naraka* (hell being).

Samu. Activities of monks and practitioners for the benefit of the temple or sangha: gardening, construction, cleaning, publishing work, etc.; sometimes called "work practice"; differs from a job in the sense that, rather than aiming to accomplish a task, it is the complement of zazen: the continuity of stillness and inner silence within activity.

Sandokai, lit. "Fusion of Difference and Sameness." Poem written by Sekito Kisen in the eighth century; one of the founding texts of Zen, recited daily in Japanese Soto monasteries; cited and commented on by many masters. It is because the many proceed from the One that differences exist. The *Sandokai* ends with this famous line: "You who seek the Way, please, do not waste the present moment."

Sangha. Assembly of monks; community of disciples; one of the "Triple Treasures" of Buddhism, along with Buddha and Dharma.

Sanshodoei, lit. "Poems on the Sansho Path." Volume of sixty-three *waka* (Japanese-style poems with five lines and thirty-one syllables: 5-7-5-7-7) composed by Master Dogen and published for the first time in 1472, over two hundred years after his death. *Sansho*, lit. "umbrella pine," is another name for Dogen's great temple, Eiheiji.

Satori. Enlightening or awakening produced by the fundamental cosmic power rather than by the ego; the actualization of *mushotoku*; not a special state of consciousness, but a return to the normal condition. In the Rinzai School, satori is the result of a successful practice and the object of a vehement quest; in the Soto School, practice itself is satori, in other words, fusion with the natural order of things.

Sawaki, Kodo (1880-1965). Great Japanese Soto master of the twentieth century and master of Taisen Deshimaru; ordained by

Master Koho Shonyu in Kyushu when he was eighteen; studied with Master Shokoku Zenko; for most of his life he eschewed temple life and traveled around Japan teaching Zen, which earned him the nickname "Homeless Kodo."

Sekito Kisen (Ch., Shih-t'ou Hsi-ch'ien, 700-790), lit. "Stonehead." Disciple of Seigen Gyoshi and master of Yakusan Igen; considered the first link in the Soto Zen lineage; author of the *Sandokai*, one of the founding texts of Soto Zen. When he died in zazen at the age of ninety, his body became mummified, and can still be seen in Japan's Sojiji Temple. A poem says, "West of the river lived Baso; south of the lake, Sekito. Men went from one to the other; whoever did not meet them lived in ignorance."

Sensei. Common Japanese term used by students to address their teachers; in Zen and the martial arts, connotes the respect and love which characterize the disciple's relationship with the master.

Seppo Gison (Ch., Hsueh-feng I-ts'un, 822-908). Ch'an master, disciple of Tokusan Senkan and master of Gensha Shibi and Unmon Bunen; entered his first monastery at the age of twelve, and lived in many during his lifetime, often assuming the role of tenzo. When he was fifty he founded his own temple on Mount Seppo, where more than fifteen-hundred monks lived.

Sesshin, lit. "to touch the mind." Period (usually between two and ten days) when the sangha comes together for intense practice focusing on zazen and *samu*.

Shankara (Skt., Shankaracharya, 788-820). Indian saint, poet and philosopher; reformist Hindu renowned for his knowledge and wisdom; founded many monasteries during his brief life.

Sheng-Yen (b. 1931). Contemporary Chinese Zen master, who received transmission in both the Soto and Rinzai lineages from masters Dong Chu and Ling Yuan, respectively; teaches in Taiwan and New York, where he is abbot of Dharma Drum

Mountain Monastery and founder of the Ch'an Meditation Center.

Shiguseiganmon. The four vows of the bodhisattva:
However innumerable sentient beings, I vow to save them all.
However inexhaustible the passions, I vow to extinguish them all.
However immeasurable the dharmas, I vow to master them all.
However incomparable the Buddha's truth, I vow to attain it.

Shiho. Transmission conferred by the master to the disciple, who is then authenticated as one of the successors of Buddha in that lineage.

Shikantaza, lit. "just sitting." The seated posture that encompasses the whole universe; does not use techniques such as breath-counting or koans.

Shiki. Phenomena; form; opposite of *ku* (emptiness), the source of *shiki*.

Shin School (Jodo-shin-shu, lit. "Authentic School of the Pure Land"). Founded by Shonin Shinran (1173-1262), for whom salvation came, not from personal effort (*jiriki*) but from "the strength of the other" (*tariki*). Shinran, who was married, was opposed to all forms of monastic life. The Shin sect, which experienced a great expansion in the thirteenth century, is still very popular in Japan. Taisen Deshimaru and Kodo Sawaki appreciated its characteristic gentleness and fervor.

Shin jin datsu raku, lit. "throwing down body and mind." Phrase pronounced by Master Nyojo during zazen and frequently repeated by Master Dogen. It perfectly describes what zazen practice is.

Shobogenzo, lit. "The Treasury of the Eye of the True Law." Master Dogen's main work, compiled in part by his disciple Ejo; the first great Buddhist text in Japanese; a dense work of inexhaustible wealth, which recounts and develops all the teachings received in China by the founder of Japanese Soto Zen. Not content to "follow the traces of ancient masters," Dogen improvises on traditional subjects with great freedom and impressive virtuosity.

Shodoka (Ch., Cheng-tao-ko), lit. "Song of Awakening." Second most important poem in Ch'an, after the *Shinjinmei*; collection of sixty-eight verses written by Master Yoka Daishi which contain the basic tenets of Ch'an.

Shomon. See *samsara.*

Shukke, lit. "one who has left home." A Zen monk or nun who is no longer a prisoner of duality and leaves behind their attachment to family, ownership and social position.

Shusso. Master's assistant during zazen or during sesshin; responsible for the proper atmosphere and order in the dojo.

Skandha. The five aggregates that form the personality: physicality, perception, awareness, concept (or action) and knowledge. Doomed to impermanence, decrepitude and death, the *skandha* are causally conditioned elements which make up the personality, and are a source of suffering as long as we are not aware of their emptiness (*ku*).

Sosan (Ch., Seng-Ts'an, d. 606). Disciple of Eka and master of Doshin; third Zen patriarch; author of the *Shinjinmei*, the first Zen text.

Sotoba (Ch., Su Tung-p'o, 1036-1101). Chinese poet, essayist, painter, calligrapher, and ordained bodhisattva.

Soto School. Zen school founded in ninth-century China by Master Tozan Ryokai (Ch., Tung-shan Liang-chieh) and his student Sozan Honjaku (Ch., Ts'ao-shan Pen-chi); also called "Silent-Enlightenment Zen" as opposed to "Contemplating-Words Zen" (Rinzai); stresses *shikantaza* rather than the koan practice essential to Rinzai. Soto was introduced to Japan by Dogen in 1227 upon his return from China. Three generations later, the school developed two branches, headquartered at Eiheiji and Sojiji, and today the superiors of these two temples take turns leading the school. Master Deshimaru and his successors are part of the Soto lineage.

Sutra. Sermon given by Buddha, reconstructed from memory by his disciple Ananda, according to tradition, during the first Buddhist Council which met in 480 BCE, just after Shakyamuni's death. The sutras usually begin with the words, "Thus have I heard." While the Hinayana sutras (*tripitaka*) came to us in their Pali or Sanskrit versions, the Mahayana sutras are mostly known to us in their Tibetan or Chinese translations.

Suzuki, D. T. (1870-1966). Buddhist scholar, translator and propagator of Zen in the West; adept of the koan method; studied Zen with Shaku Soen and his descendant, Sokatsu Shaku, who asked him to translate Zen texts into English for the scholarly readership.

Swami Prabhavanda (1893-1976). Contemporary Hindu monk; member of the Ramakrishna Order of India; author of numerous works on the spiritual traditions of India; founder of the Vedanta Society of Southern California.

Tanden. See *hara.*

Tanka Tennen (Ch., Tan-hsia T'ien-jan, 739-824). Disciple of Sekito Kisen, then of Baso; friend of layman P'ang. At the age of eighty, after a life marked by anti-conformist behavior, he founded a monastery on Mount Tanka, where he had a following of three hundred monks.

Tenno Dogo (Ch., T'ien-huang Tao-wu, 738-807). Ch'an master, disciple of Sekito Kisen and master of Ryutan Soshin.

Tenzo, lit. "kitchen master." Cook in a temple or monastery; a very important person in Zen; hero of many stories and anecdotes. Great masters such as Isan, Tozan and Seppo served as tenzo. The tenzo's role was the subject of a text by Master Dogen entitled *Tenzo Kyokun* ("Instructions for the Tenzo").

Tokujo (Sensu) (eighth-ninth centuries). Disciple of Yakusan Igen and master of Kassan Zen'e.

Tokusan Senkan (Ch., Te-shan Hsuan-chien, 781-867). Disciple of Ryutan Soshin and master of Seppo Gison; scholar renowned for his knowledge of the *Diamond Sutra* who burned all his books to follow the Way and dedicate himself to the practice of zazen; famous for his educational method christened *bokatsu* (from *bo*, "stick," and *katsu*, "shout").

Tozan Ryokai (Ch., Tung-shan Liang-chieh, 807-869). Disciple of Ungan Donjo and master of Ungo Doyo, among others; founder, with Sozan Honjaku, of the Soto School; author of the *Hokyozanmai*, one of the founding Zen texts, still recited in Japanese monasteries.

Ungan Donjo (Ch., Yun-yen T'an-sheng, 781-841). Disciple of Yakusan Igen and master of Tozan Ryokai. After the death of his first teacher, Hyakujo Ekai, Ungan studied with Yakusan and eventually became his successor. He then went to live on Mount Ungan, "Cloud Cliff."

Ungo Doyo (Ch., Yun-chu Tao-ying, d. 902). Disciple of Tozan Ryokai, he continued the Soto lineage founded by his master.

Vasubandhu (fourth-fifth centuries). Twenty-first patriarch of the Indian Zen lineage; scholar and author of commentaries on Mahayana texts such as the *Diamond Sutra* and *Lotus Sutra*.

Wanshi Shogaku (Ch., Hung-chih Cheng-chueh, 1091-1157). Disciple of Tanka Shijun; reputed Chinese Soto master greatly admired by Dogen; known for his pointed debates with Rinzai master Daie Soko (Ch., Ta-hui Tsung-kao) on the advantages of Soto's "*mokusho* Zen" ("silent sitting Zen"), as compared to Rinzai's "*kanna* Zen" ("spoken Zen," or "koan Zen"); author of the first *Zazenshin*, which would later be adapted by Dogen.

Yoka Daishi (or Genkaku, Ch., Yung-chia Hsuan-chueh, 665-713). Disciple of Eno, the sixth patriarch; nicknamed "One-

Night Satori" in reference to his brief encounter with Eno, after which the latter confirmed his awakening; author of the *Shodoka*, one of the four oldest Zen texts.

Zafu. Round cushion filled with kapok used for sitting zazen; modeled on the grass cushion on which Shakyamuni had his satori.

Zazen. Zen meditation practice; sitting with legs crossed and back straight on a zafu, facing the wall in the Soto tradition and facing the center of the dojo in the Rinzai tradition. Breathing is slow and deep, the mind observes thoughts without following or rejecting them. See also *hishiryo, mushotoku, shikantaza* and *shin jin datsu raku*.

Zazenshin, lit. "Needle of Zazen." Poem on the meaning of zazen, the essence of the Dharma, written by Wanshi Shogaku in the twelfth century and later commented on and reworked by Master Dogen in the *Shobogenzo*.

Index

197

Index of Zen Stories